Idea Hacks

Come up with 10X More Creative Ideas in 1/2 the Time

By I. C. Robledo

www.Amazon.com/author/icrobledo

Idea Hacks: Come up with 10X More Creative Ideas in 1/2 the Time

Table of Contents

What are "Idea Hacks"?

Idea hacks are systems that help you to come up with creative ideas with much less effort. I've had my share of difficulties and blocks when trying to come up with new ideas, and so I came up with hacks, or shortcuts, to overcome those problems. With idea hacks, you can come up with new ideas regardless of whether you feel mentally blocked or demotivated. Even if you feel bored, uninspired, or if you are trapped at home on a rainy day, idea hacks provide you with a shortcut that will help you to come up with ideas right away.

The above paragraph is a very brief overview of what idea hacks are. There are actually many other important concepts to cover before we go into greater detail about idea hacks, and how to use them. Now I will tell you everything you need to know before you can get the best use from them.

If you are eager to learn about idea hacks immediately, you may skip forward to the "Idea Hacks" section. Be sure to return and read the first part of the book later, though. It is very important.

Also, this book has a bonus at the end, of "101 Creative Exercises to Try". You may explore them at any time.

The Reason for Idea Hacks

Most people need a stimulus from the environment in order to create. **A stimulus is anything that gives you the idea to create something new.** It may be a muse, a chance inspirational event, beautiful scenery, or something else. Instead of relying on a random stimulus, truly creative people have a way of actually *becoming* the stimulus themselves. They learn to create as they need to, whether or not there is any stimulus available. For these highly creative people, the process of creating becomes internalized. They become creative generators themselves, able to come up with ideas as they please. This is one of the highest states of creativity which tends to remain out of reach for many.

But we have to ask, why do most of us *need* stimuli to create? What if we can learn to be like the most creative people, and become the stimulation for ideas ourselves, without needing outside influence? Because of such questions, the vast majority of the idea hacks in this book are dedicated to coming up with ideas with no outside stimulation. This is powerful because you won't need to be visited by the muse, to see the beautiful sunset or butterfly, or to experience lively artwork in order to create. Everything that you already need will come from inside. This is possible with idea hacks.

Idea hacks are powerful tools you can use to come up with creative ideas in any situation. These systems are built for those who prefer to rely on themselves rather than to wait for something or someone else to inspire them to create. If you are interested in creating on your own terms, and becoming your own stimulus for new ideas, you are reading the right book.

Creative Ideas Are for Everyone

It's Not Just for the Chosen Few – It's for You and Me Too

Many people have the wrong idea about what it means to be creative.

Whenever the topic of creativity comes up, I sense hesitation and sometimes even fear in many people. Often, I'm left with the impression that people think creativity is for someone else. It's for other people who were born with the gift, not them. They think it's for the artist, the writer, the inventor, the highly intelligent, the wealthy, and so forth.

The idea comes out that you can't be creative unless you have all of the right materials. They say you can't be creative unless you have the money to buy the best stuff. You can't be creative unless it runs in your family, as if there were a creative gene.... There are too many "You can't be creative unless..." type of statements, and many of us assume it isn't for us.

The problem with this thinking is it is completely wrong.

Actually, creativity is for people like you and me. Whether you are white collar or blue collar, in a creative profession or not, from a creative family or not, creativity is for you. You can implement it in your job, with your family, with a hobby, in solving general problems, and in many other cases too.

And if you say to me, "You don't know me, I'm simply not creative. I've tried", then I'll ask you to give me a chance to help you. Just read this book and give the systems I offer a try. You will lose nothing from giving it a chance, but you may gain the ability to tap into your creative potential if you read and apply the idea hacks described. Keep in mind that you don't need to have a particular background. Regardless of your profession, education, or understanding of how creativity works, this book will help you create an abundance of new ideas in a way that you never have.

3

The Boy Who Harnessed the Wind

Here is a compelling example of someone who didn't let barriers get in the way of his creativity. You probably have never heard of him, an African boy from Malawi named William Kamkwamba.

As a boy, he was dedicated to going to school to get his education. However, because he didn't have the $80 to pay an annual fee, he was forced to drop out in his freshman year of high school. Even with this major setback, he was still dedicated to learning. He went to the library and came across a beginner's physics textbook, where he saw diagrams of windmills. The book itself was in English, a foreign language for him. Nonetheless, he decided he wanted to build his own windmill, to help bring electric power to his small village, which lacked this energy source.

With great persistence, he built his own version of a windmill from scraps of wire, an old bicycle hub, and flattened PVC pipe for blades. With virtually no resources, a lack of formal education, no guidance or help, and living in poverty, he succeeded in making a windmill that would power a few lightbulbs, charge cell phones, and operate a water pump for his home and the small village he lived in. Although these things may seem minimal to many of us, his creative ability and persistence made a big difference to many lives.

To learn more about William Kamkwamba's life, you may wish to read *The Boy Who Harnessed the Wind*.

The point is this boy made a major creative contribution to his family and his village with practically no resources. And his case may be extreme, but I have often heard of cases where people come up with creative solutions even in situations that seem hopeless. You don't necessarily need ideal circumstances in order to create. For some people, a lack of the "right" materials and resources is not enough to hold them back.

I already stated this, but it's an important point. This book is here to help you create, regardless of resources, time, income, or background. William Kamkwamba is a living example that you do not need a perfect environment, wealth, or the best resources in order to create. Motivation alone can be a good starting point.

You may think William Kamkwamba is a special case, and most of us would not be capable of his achievements. Of course, we may not accomplish exactly what he did, but we still have much creative potential inside that we often fail to use. I will show you why and how we all have this ability, and help draw out your creativity so you can come up with more ideas than you even need.

Who is This Book for?

If You Feel Discouraged

Perhaps you have tried getting creative in the past. You may have come up with many ideas that were rejected or maybe even made fun of. You desperately want to get new ideas and make something of your own, but as time passes you feel that this is less and less likely. Lack of time, not knowing where to begin, and a bad track record when you have tried have all left you feeling discouraged, uncertain if you were meant to be creative at all.

The way to get over this feeling is to keep things simple, and focus on gathering new ideas, which is what this book is all about. To begin, the goal needs to be to come up with many, many ideas. When you have success with this, you will regain the confidence you need to carry through on your creative plans.

If You Have Trouble Starting Creative Projects

Many creative people start with a dream of something they want to make happen. But perhaps you don't have a well-developed dream that you want to carry out. Maybe you are attracted to the idea of making something new, and you aren't sure yet of the specific direction you should go in, or where to even get the ideas to start figuring this out. The idea of starting without any kind of plan is probably overwhelming, and so you set your creative wishes aside. In time, unfortunately it becomes too easy to forget about your creative aspirations.

Having trouble getting started is fairly common. In fact, it can be one of the more difficult parts of getting creative. I've noticed that even the most creative people tend to need a topic or some kind of direction in order to start producing ideas. If you ask a creative person to "do something creative", you may be surprised that this can have poor results. But it's like asking a bilingual person to "say something in your language". It can actually be easy to freeze up when the possibilities are endless. This book will help you to get more specific, which will help you to produce more ideas in the directions that interest you.

If You Have Trouble Coming Up With Ideas on Your Own

You may find that sometimes you are able to come up with some ideas, but you are concerned that you tend to need more help than you would like. Perhaps you rely heavily on team brainstorming sessions, or you simply call a "creative friend" who can give you plenty of ideas to start with. The problem with looking to others for assistance is that later on you are left wondering if any of the ideas are really your own. You will grow concerned about whether you are simply working on others' creative plans, rather than coming up with your own unique ideas.

This book will provide you with systems so you do not need to rely on anyone else to help you come up with ideas. Even if you do brainstorming sessions or bounce ideas off of other creative people, you will feel more prepared by bringing your own creative ideas to share first.

If You Sometimes Have a Mental Block or Fall into a Creative Slump

Perhaps you are already a creative person with your own unique ideas and contributions. Well, blocks among even creative people are fairly common. You have probably heard of writer's block or artist's block, for example. These can happen for many reasons... losing interest in your topic, overreliance on a muse or inspiration, putting too much pressure on yourself, and so forth.

Sometimes you simply fall into a creative slump – you start a project excited, but soon run out of ideas, and you aren't sure how to get those creative juices flowing again. Perhaps many new challenges pop up that you didn't expect, and you become overwhelmed. The project runs into problem after problem, and you need more and more ideas. Unsure how to get so many ideas, you lose the excitement, become frustrated, and wonder if the project is worth continuing.

You'll know when you are in a slump or feeling the mental block. It often feels like you are drawing a blank, or like you have tunnel vision. It becomes hard to imagine much else besides this blank, this nothing-ness, once it takes over. And then the fear sets in that you will not be able to create anything this time, that you will never have another good idea. And when this fear sets in, it will only make you freeze up, and make it even less likely for you to come up with more ideas.

But of course, *you will have more ideas.* The systems in this book are designed to make these mental blocks a thing of the past. The best thing to do when you are blocked is to use idea hacks to make the ideas come out as fast as you can. This will prove that you are not truly blocked, and you will be ready to move on and get creative again.

If You Want a Proven System to Help Come Up With Ideas

Creativity is a misunderstood concept. Even people who are themselves creative, such as artists, musicians, and entrepreneurs, often have misguided ideas about it. Some of them may rely on a muse, on inspiration, ingenious insights and breakthroughs, or instinct. These are all usable, but waiting for unreliable bursts of inspiration will not help you in coming up with creative ideas when you really need them.

If you want to be truly creative, you have to have a system that allows you to be creative regardless of circumstance. Ideally, you would want multiple systems you can use in a variety of situations, which is what this book provides. The systems are simple to learn and highly effective. This way, for those of us who want something actionable to increase our creativity, rather than vague statements or advice, this book should put us onto the path to make this happen.

Before You Continue . . .

As a thank you for reading, I want you to have a free guide called:

Step Up Your Learning: Free Tools to Learn Almost Anything

Have you ever wondered what the best sites and resources for learning are? It takes time and effort to figure out which sites are worth it and which are not. I hope to save you some of that time so you can spend more of it learning instead of searching the Internet.

In the past ten years or so, there has been a free learning revolution happening. More and more resources for learning are becoming available to the public at no cost. With so many new ones coming out, it's easy to miss out on some of the great learning opportunities available. Fortunately for you, this guide is short at around 4,000 words, and tells you exactly what you need to know.

The guide stems from my own experiences of using a variety of learning sites and resources. In it, you will discover the best places to go for learning at no cost. Also, I'll explain which resources are best for you, depending on your learning goals.

You can download this free guide as a PDF by typing this website into your browser:

http://bit.ly/Robledo

Now, let's get back on topic.

Am I the Right Person to Discuss Creativity?

This may surprise you, but I have never viewed myself as especially creative. The times I did decide to create something, it tended to be a struggle. What drove me to write this book was noticing that I wanted to be creative, but I didn't seem to have a talent for it. I realized this was a skill I would need to develop.

In fact, if we look at two opposite spectrums, of analytic ability, and of creative ability, I would say I was far stronger at being analytical. For example, this would mean being good at finding the one correct solution on a standardized test such as the SAT or GRE, or on most exams. But then again, our educational system prepares us for being analytical, whereas it doesn't spend much energy on our creative sides. I'm actually not sure that any of us is naturally analytical or creative. I think both styles require some amount of training or preparation.

Many of us spend little to no time developing our creative selves. In that case, we shouldn't be at all surprised if we lack creative abilities. To improve in this ability, we need to actually use our creative skills, and practice coming up with new ideas.

I believe I am the right person to discuss the topic because I made the conscious choice to improve my creative abilities. I noticed when using certain systems, coming up with even hundreds of ideas was not especially difficult. At that point I realized these idea hacks were something that could be helpful to others, if I found them so useful.

After I came up with a few idea hacks, I brainstormed creatively, using my own systems to come up with more and more systems, until I came up with all of the systems in this book. Now, I call these systems "idea hacks" because they can be used to generate ideas quite rapidly. It will become rather easy to come up with a hundred or more ideas in a day, which I think is an excellent start for any creative project. The best part is they are simple for anyone to use.

Let's go deeper into my background with creativity. The point of the following is to show how creativity can evolve throughout a life, and to support that my creative background gives me the expertise to cover this topic. Also, I would like you to reflect on your own creative past and see what you can learn from your past experiences. Here is a brief summary of my creative life.

At four years old, my first memory is of waking up and going to the kitchen table. My grandfather was there, and he asked me what I dreamt. I didn't know what a dream was, so he explained that it was those things which happen to you in the night when you are sleeping. I understood, and I realized for the first time that there is a difference between the imagination (or the dream world), and the waking world. I think now that the first basic step of creativity for a child is simply to realize that creations and reality are different things. As a very young child, creative energy is reckless and uncontrollable – we create, as in dreams, without even knowing we are creating. But as adults, we can learn to control this energy and be productive with it.

Around four or five, some of my earliest memories are of being terribly frightened. There were people around, sometimes monsters that didn't belong, that I knew shouldn't be there. To explain it, I saw creatures and things appear in the night when it was dark. I would explain it now like a Rorschach test. This is the classic inkblot test, with no clearly formed objects in them, but the vague figures (left by ink marks) are often enough to get people to "see" things in them. One person may see a crab, the other may see his grandmother.

In the dark night, I saw different shades of black or gray and patterns everywhere I looked. Somehow, my mind must have turned every vague pattern into a concrete object or person. But it was more complex than that. They came to life in such vivid detail and they could move. For instance, I once saw Superman fly right over my head. I knew these things shouldn't be there, but I couldn't understand it, and they scared me at the time. Now, I would explain it as an overactive imagination, coming from a child with much creative potential, perhaps.

Skip forward to around seven years old, and I was completely obsessed with wanting to drive. If my mother were to leave me alone in the car, I would inevitably move the steering wheel, hit any buttons, and on more than one occasion I hit the gas pedal and flooded the engine so it wouldn't start for a while. Of course, she was very wise to have taken the keys with her, or I might have been tempted to take it for a ride.

The obsession didn't end there. I would pretend nonstop that I was driving. I had a Frisbee and I would act as if it were a steering wheel, and I would "drive" around the house. Sometimes, I would even grab a coat hanger and do the same thing. Whenever my mother drove, I paid attention to how she handled the car. I knew about the gas, the brakes, and I noticed how much she had to turn the wheel to make a given turn. Of course, I applied all of this knowledge during my pretend driving sessions. If you had asked me what I wanted to do when I grew up, I probably would have said I wanted to be a racecar driver. This seems like a normal level of creativity for the age.

By around ten, eleven, twelve, things have changed. I recall being very uncomfortable with creating something of my own. By this point, I don't think I was creating anything unless it was required by a class, but even there it was somewhat of a rarity. I tended to worry too much about doing something wrong. On one occasion for my sixth grade class we were supposed to make up a song and sing it in front of the class. I would probably have rather done anything else instead of this, by this age. I worked on the project with a friend and we wrote a rap song. It wasn't very good, but the expectations didn't seem high for it either. I will discuss a bit later in the book why unfortunately it is common for children to lose creativity as they get older.

Skip to around eighteen and nineteen, and I had become obsessive with documenting every poetic thought I could. Having had no training in how to do this, perhaps some of it was bad, but I think some of it was decent. It was an interesting time because it was a sort of mad explosion of creativity. For everything that happened, even if it was nothing, I tried to wrestle a poem out of it. Some of it was about the universe, women, or my general life at the time as a university student.

I also ended up with a partly sketched idea for a film around the time. I even bought a book on how to write a screenplay, but nothing ever came of it.

A few years later I was researching creativity while working on my master's degree in industrial-organizational psychology. Much of my focus was spent on researching techniques which could help to improve creativity. I have authored or co-authored fourteen academic publications, in journals such as *Creativity Research Journal* and *Journal of Organizational Behavior*. And I was the primary author of the conclusion chapter of the "Handbook of Organizational Creativity".

From there, skip to around twenty-six to twenty-eight, and I was collecting piles and piles of ideas for possible fiction books and short stories to write. I started to find that at times there could be a frenzy of ideas. I sometimes went through a full yellow pad notebook in a matter of hours, filling it with ideas for characters, plots, settings, themes, and so forth. At other times, there was a void of creativity, and I was unable to come up with anything.

Now in the present time, I use most of my creative energy on coming up with ideas for nonfiction books, such as for chapters, sections, topics, titles, and so forth. Also, I operate my own independent author business. For example, I am writer, marketer, and make final choices on cover designs or whether a book will be translated or provided in paper or audio formats. Much of my creative energy is spent on coming up with book ideas or ideas to improve the business or marketing in some way. And of course, recently, I have been coming up with creative systems or idea hacks to help everyone come up with more ideas.

There have been periods of high levels of creativity in my life, but it was never well-sustained until the past few years, when I decided to come up with systems to get creative whenever I felt I needed to. For every period of great windfalls of creativity, I remember agonizing, sometimes falling into dark moods, just drawing a blank, completely lacking any direction. Again, this is the reason I came up with the systems in this book. And although my creativity has been mostly centered on writing fiction and nonfiction and on ideas for improving my writing business, the idea hacks can be applied to any other topic you wish to create in.

How Much are Ideas Worth?

Perspective 1: Ideas are Worthless

Note that I do not think ideas are worthless, but I want to discuss this perspective to get us thinking critically about what ideas are worth. Also, this is a true perspective I have sometimes heard from people who do not think ideas have much value.

Let's begin with the points someone would make with this perspective, of thinking ideas are not worth anything. Here is what they might say:

You have to ask yourself, where do ideas come from? Who has them? They can come from pretty much anyone, anywhere. This could be children, amateurs, people who have no knowledge on a topic, people with no practical experience, or chronic complainers who never take action. So if ideas are so easy to come across from people with no real authority, they must not be worth very much.

Another problem with ideas is that hardly anyone seems to take action on the ideas they do have. Many people, even when they have good ideas, end up talking about them more than actually putting them into action. To make matters worse, the *Psychological Science* article, "When Intentions Go Public", by Peter Gollwitzer and his colleagues, has shown that talking about future plans tends to make you feel as if you have already met your goal. Because of this, those who talk about their ideas will be less likely to make them into a reality. This sort of trend makes it seem like ideas have no value.

As a final point, most ideas are not very good. For every idea to start Facebook or Microsoft, or to create the *Mona Lisa*, there are probably thousands of other ideas which were horrible. The vast majority of ideas are hopelessly bad and destined to fail. Why would anyone want to work on coming up with ideas, when most of them will not succeed? Isn't our time better spent in other ways, instead of on ideas?

Perspective 2: Ideas Have Resulted in the Greatest Inventions and Creations – They Have the Potential to Result in Something Priceless and Timeless

Again, I do not agree with perspective 1, but it does raise some interesting points that we should consider. I think by looking at perspective 1 seriously, we will be in a better position to see the value of perspective 2.

In perspective 1 it was said that everyone has ideas, even people with no authority, so they can't possibly be worth much. It's true that pretty much anyone can have ideas. But most people settle for basic and common ones. They do not typically invest in their ability to come up with more and better ideas, which is what we will set out to do in this book. Since many people hold perspective 1, or for a variety of reasons they simply don't exercise their ability to come up with ideas, the ones who take them seriously will have fairly little competition. Allow others to come up with no or few worthy ideas. But with the right systems, you can generate hundreds of them and find the ones that are worth investing your time in. Ultimately, this will help you to accomplish your creative goals.

The other point was that hardly anyone takes action on their ideas, making them just a waste of time and useless. This may be true as well. It's human nature to want to discuss ideas and sometimes even brag about interesting ones that we come up with. If you've ever heard someone go on about how they were the first person to come up with the idea for the internet, or a search engine, or they had an idea for an app but someone else made it first, you know that people tend to entertain themselves by discussing such topics. It's fun, it interests people, and they might even be congratulated for having a good idea. Well, the point is true that many people spend more time talking than acting on their ideas. But being aware of this fact can help you to become the exception. You can choose to act on your best ideas. You may even make a rule if you find yourself talking too much instead of taking action. You can decide that for every minute you spend talking, you have to spend five minutes on making your idea into a reality.

The last point in perspective 1 was that most ideas are not very good. This is also true. The point of coming up with ideas, however, is not for all of them to be great. No one, not even the most brilliant creators, has all great ideas. Instead, it is important to push through, coming up with more and more ideas until you hit upon the right one. It's perfectly fine to come up with a hundred ideas and to have one or two excellent ones come out of it. The trick then is to come up with ideas fast, so you can move on to the next creative steps of putting your best ideas into action.

An analogy I like to use is that coming up with good ideas is like mining for gold. Sure, most of what you find won't be gold, and it won't be even a bit valuable. But every once in a while you will hit upon a brilliant and shiny object, "gold", or a great idea, which will make the whole process worthwhile. Imagine if you came up with a thousand ideas. Perhaps one or two of those would give you a major breakthrough. A thousand ideas may sound like a huge amount, but it isn't that big of a price to pay if one of those helps to radically change your life or the lives of others.

What is Creativity?

Most of us have a good general idea of what creativity is, but given that there are often misconceptions about creativity, I think this would be a good time to go over exactly what it means.

First off, a reminder. Many of us automatically think of artists, musicians, or perhaps inventors when we think of creativity. And these are all great examples. But there is no reason others cannot be creative: a computer engineer, a chef, an architect, a gardener, a salesperson, and so forth. Creative hobbies are an obvious point of creativity, but creativity is something that can be applied in a variety of industries and for a variety of purposes. One key place is in solving problems. The more ideas you can come up with, the more likely you are to solve a difficult creative problem.

Now, to define what creativity is, it is made up of two key parts. These are originality and usefulness. These will be further explained on the next page.

Originality

This book will focus on helping you come up with new ideas, which is the originality part of creativity. To figure out if something is original, ask the following questions.

Stage 1: Is the idea new to you?

The first stage of originality is when something is new to you. You come up with an idea and it's the first time you've ever heard of it. For example, you come up with the idea to make a company built around providing hair products just for dogs. It involves combs, shampoos, conditioners, shaving gear, and instructional videos on how to give the dog a bath, and so forth.

This is the first stage of originality. Many people get excited at their new idea, and they think this is all they need. It's new, it's original, and they assume it's creative. Actually, we will have to examine it more thoroughly to see just how original (or creative) it really is.

Stage 2: Is the idea new to the general population?

Okay, so the idea may be new to you. This is a big step. But is it new to anyone else? Has anyone else started a company using this idea? Has anyone else patented items related to this? Is anyone else talking about it? If you search the internet, are there websites dedicated to the topic?

If you do some research and you can't find anything about it anywhere, then you have a highly original idea. In this case, a quick search found a variety of products and services of the type I mentioned. So although the idea may have been original to me, it probably wasn't very original to the general population.

I used this type of example on purpose, though, because it provides us with a lesson. Even if it turns out that other people came up with an idea before you, if the idea was original to you, then it still counts as stage 1 originality. This is because it took some of your creative energy to come up with it. However, you should realize that some ideas original to you may not be original for others. Unfortunately, stage 1 originality doesn't count for much, other than to acknowledge you have put your creative energy to use in coming up with something new for yourself. Stage 2 originality will be much more important to achieve.

In history, there are various cases of people with highly original discoveries or creations, but they were just a bit too late in showing their work to the public. For example. Charles Darwin and Alfred Wallace both discovered evolution within a few years of each other in the 1850s, independently. And Isaac Newton and Gottfried Leibniz both discovered Calculus, again within several years of each other in the mid-1600s, independently. These were obviously original and creative ideas, but the first person to make his ideas clear and public was the one who got most of the credit. In these cases, Darwin and Newton, respectively. What is seen as original is constantly changing, as people are exposed to new work. Something can be original one day, but become unoriginal if you wait even just one day!

Stage 3: Is the idea new to everyone?

This would be the third stage of originality, to come up with an idea that is new to everyone. This would mean no one at any other place or at any time in history had ever had the idea. This is interesting to consider, but of course we can never prove if this happens. Stage 3 creativity will have to be a dream or a theoretical idea for most of us, because we can never know for sure if we have achieved it. For practical purposes, stage 2 originality is the highest level of originality you should concern yourself with.

The point of stage 3 originality is just for you to understand that we can never be 100% sure someone else hasn't had the same idea. For example, perhaps someone discovered calculus two thousand years ago and had the full concept in their mind, but then was struck by lightning and never put it on paper. Or perhaps they did document it but the book was destroyed in history. It's very unlikely, but not impossible.

Unoriginal ideas can still be used creatively

I'm sure this sounds strange, but it's important to make the point that you can still use unoriginal ideas creatively. So, a lack of original ideas isn't necessarily an excuse for not being creative.

For example, let's take the dog haircare business I mentioned above. As mentioned, these types of products are already available on the internet. So the core idea is not original, but originality is just something new. If we modify an unoriginal idea to create something new, then it becomes original. In this case, what if we turn it into a service. You simply go door to door offering to groom any animals in the home. This service could pride itself on its speed and high quality. I don't know if that idea is being done or not, but the point is you can always make modifications to ideas until you come up with something original to the public. Another option would be to create new formulas for the shampoos and conditioners used, making them original. If you believe in an idea, I would caution you against giving up on it too easily. Some minor adjustments may be all you need to create something new and better than the current options.

I felt the need to mention this because often, people tend to assume if you start out with an idea which has "been done before", that this automatically means you have a bad idea or that it isn't worth doing, and this is not necessarily true. Sometimes, less original ideas are actually better, because people are more familiar with them. A new soda with extra salt, hot sauce, and soy sauce may be original, but it's not likely to be very successful. Just because something is very high or low on originality, doesn't say much as to whether it will succeed or not. That has to do with the usefulness or quality, which is the next part of creativity.

Usefulness (or Quality)

Does your idea solve a problem?

Many people think creative ideas are mostly about originality. It's true that originality is a key part of creativity, but originality alone isn't enough to make something creative. If something is very high on originality, and low on quality, we tend to call it bizarre. Think of my soda example above with extra salt, hot sauce, and soy sauce. Most people probably wouldn't want to try it, because it is quite strange and unexpected for a soda.

In artistic paintings or novel-writing, the most critical element as to whether something is creative or not, tends to be in its originality. For that reason, many of us might assume originality is the most important part of creativity. But you must understand that usefulness is actually just as important as originality. Usefulness is something that matters more in other kinds of creative endeavors, such as starting a new company, solving a creative problem, or designing a new product. These are all areas where people will not be interested in solutions which have no practical use.

To gauge usefulness, you have to ask if your idea is a relevant response to the problem. Sometimes, people think they are being creative because they came up with a wild response. But if it doesn't actually help to solve the problem or get the outcomes you are looking for, then it isn't truly creative.

Here is a brief overview of what different levels of originality and quality mean:

<u>High quality</u> and <u>high originality</u> ➜ you have a creative solution

<u>High quality</u> and <u>low originality</u> ➜ you have a good solution, but not creative

<u>Low quality</u> and <u>high originality</u> ➜ you have a bizarre "solution", unlikely to be effective

<u>Low quality</u> and <u>low originality</u> ➜ you have a poor solution and it is not creative

Why Creativity Matters

Fun

Personally, I find creating new things fun. It is a chance to do something new, different, make something up and share it with people. Then, if it goes well they get to have fun with the creation or put it to use in some way.

Many people may not feel the need to be creative just to have fun. After all, there are other ways to do this, like watching movies, playing video games, board games, biking, sports, taking pictures, and so forth. But getting creative lets us have fun in a different way, where you become the person who is making up something new for others to enjoy.

Personally, I don't make the choice between having fun through hobbies and having fun through creating. I like to have both options open.

Fight Boredom... by Getting Bored

"You get ideas from daydreaming. You get ideas from being bored.
You get ideas all the time. The only difference between writers and
other people is we notice when we're doing it."

– Neil Gaiman, fantasy & sci-fi author

Neil Gaiman (from the above quote) has said that when he wants to
create something, he forces himself to get really, really bored. I thought
this was interesting when I first heard about it. It was interesting
enough that I gave it some thought, and I wondered why being bored
would help for getting creative. But it's actually pretty straightforward.
Creativity is the mind's natural way of dealing with boredom. Boredom
is what happens when there is a lack of stimulation, and a lack of anything new or interesting. Well, creativity introduces new stimulation,
and gives us new and interesting things to think about and deal with.
Think of creativity like antibodies that attack boredom, much like they
help attack viruses that try to enter our bodies.

Also, consider this. When do people become creative in general, in so-
cieties? It happens when they have all of their basic needs met. For example, they have clean water, food, their civilization is at peace or an
army of elite warriors is handling any possible threats. For instance,
consider the Renaissance period in Europe that started around 1350
and lasted until around 1600. Before this "rebirth" period that was
bursting with creativity, there were the Dark Ages, a period character-
ized by war, famine, and disease. It seems like no coincidence that as
those burdens began to fade, the Renaissance began to blossom.

Now in the more developed countries, people are generally healthy,
and do not need to be worried about dying from war or famine. Of
course, not everyone today is in this circumstance, but much of the
more creative areas are in such a beneficial situation. My belief is that
when all basic needs are met, life becomes relatively easy. Boredom
begins to set in. The natural defense mechanism for boredom then begins to kick in, and creativity blooms for many people. Not everyone
will necessarily be bored or creative, but overall, there is much more
creativity during these conditions.

People need something to occupy their minds with. You can be occupied with other people's problems, with other people's creations (such as movies and television), or with your own creations. Either way, the mind requires some kind of stimulation. Getting creative is just an interesting route to go because you call the shots, you control the direction, and you aren't simply tackling all of the problems someone else told you were important to look into. You are looking into your own endeavors, and taking the best course of action you see fit.

I feel the need to mention that those in very tough circumstances are sometimes surprisingly creative as well – Remember William Kamkwamba who built a windmill with virtually no resources. Something about the *need* to improve things tends to motivate people to find creative solutions to tough problems.

Here is another example of how creativity can arise out of need, rather than ideal conditions.

Some years ago, I was told the story of a bully in high school who insisted that another boy, who was much smaller in size, meet him for a fight after school. The bully showed up at the meeting point under a tree and waited. The other boy hadn't arrived yet, and no one was around. Not even a moment passed, and the bully was knocked to the ground, taking punches from all sides. The fight was over quite fast. The winner was the smaller boy who had been bullied.

What is the explanation? The boy who was bullied into fighting spent some time wondering how he could possibly win a fight against this larger, tougher opponent. After some thought, he came to the creative solution that he would arrive at the meeting point ahead of time, climb a tree nearby and hide. When the moment was right, he would jump down surprising the bully, and attack him relentlessly. The plan worked because he was in a situation where it absolutely had to work. To fail would have meant to lose the fight and probably get seriously injured. His creativity helped him avoid this fate.

Professional Advancement

Whatever your work environment, the more ideas you are able to come up with, the more likely you will be able to discover a great idea that helps you to make a breakthrough. Also, those who are able to be more creative in their work will often be more likely to advance in position.

Unfortunately, not all work environments are friendly toward new ideas. Some creatives will feel trapped in systems that restrict them and do not let their creative energies free. They may get stuck in work environments that do not suit their abilities or care for what they are able to create. Many workplaces will simply want you to produce, and to do as you are told, which is not ideal for those who wish to pursue the creative path.

The good news is you are not trapped. You may feel trapped temporarily, but creativity offers a way out of this.

Sometimes none of your available options will seem to fit what you are looking for. Consider that perhaps the ideal path you want for yourself doesn't exist yet, and you will need to create it. If you feel restricted by your current setting and the actions you are allowed to pursue, the creative option of going your own way may be the best solution to building the life you want.

Of course, if you are in a work environment that understands your wishes to be more creative in the workplace, you may pursue your creative goals there without needing to pursue a completely independent path.

Have New & Interesting Things to Talk About

The creative person will be better at coming up with new things to talk about as a conversation grows stale. Some people criticize small talk because it is often predictable and boring. There are only so many conversations about the time, weather, or "what do you do" that people care to have. The creative person is able to find new topics to discuss which are interesting, or is able to put a new spin on some of these common small-talk topics.

I used to suffer with this syndrome of finding it difficult to keep a conversation flow moving (I still do sometimes), but working on your creative abilities can help strongly with this. It can also help with your sense of humor or your ability to connect topics even if they seem unrelated. This will keep things interesting and make you a more entertaining person to be around.

Become More Self-Reliant

Often, we don't have all of the tools or resources that we would ideally need to solve a problem. The creative person is able to come up with ideas to solve problems and to put them into action, even if they don't seem to have all of the necessary resources.

Consider a painter who needs red paint for his work of art. Unfortunately, there has been a mistake and none of the art shops are carrying the color right now. The artist can give up and decide he will have to work without red paint, or he can search for some kind of alternative. Perhaps he can mix other colors to create his own red paint (actually this would work for other colors, but since red is a primary color, no two other colors would mix to create red). Or perhaps he can find some ketchup or food coloring, possibly mixing it with something else to create the right texture. Not to get gory, but another option is to prick his finger and use his own blood as paint, if he is really desperate.

As another example of how creativity is good for self-reliance, consider the question: How would you fix a pair of eyeglasses if you didn't have a miniature flathead screwdriver?

What if you have a steel paperclip and a hammer? What would you do then? A solution could be to hammer the tip of the paperclip, which will flatten it, giving you a flat screwdriver head. This of course will allow you to use it as a small screwdriver, and fix your glasses. This is the type of response that allows creatives to become more self-reliant.

Come Up with Solutions to Tough Problems

As you expand your creative abilities, you will tend to value your ability to come up with ideas in tough situations. You will be more likely to "think on your feet" and come up with useful solutions, whereas someone else may freeze up, not sure how to make progress. Knowing how to come up with ideas when you need them will give you extra confidence in new situations. You will be able to tell yourself that you have faced rough situations before, and you successfully came up with good ideas to solve the problem. And you will realize that you are prepared to do the same in this case as well.

We all occasionally have difficult problems of our own to solve, but of course, we are facing a time when there are a wide variety of tough world problems as well. My goal here isn't to solve them, but to point out that we have no shortage of challenging problems.

There are many big world issues to deal with, and most of them could be helped by creative thinking. To name some:

- Global warming

- Energy crises

- Pollution

- Poverty

- Animal endangerment

- Lack of quality healthcare

- Lack of quality education

Surely, there are many other significant issues as well. This is just a small sampling of them. Tough problems are big enough that they are tackled by large governments, businesses, and volunteer organizations. However, individuals should not discount themselves so easily. Remember the story of William Kamkwamba and the windmill. He helped bring a significant energy source to his own village despite a lack of education, resources, and living in poverty.

31

Anyone is capable of joining the effort to come up with more ideas to solve these problems and to help humanity make progress. When you have a powerful idea, you will attract others like a magnet, and they will want to join in and help make your idea a reality. Actually, this is what has happened with William Kamkwamba. His ideas and his work ethic have attracted investors around the world to want to work with him on larger projects.

What is the Creative Process?

Now that you know creativity is made up of original and useful solutions, let's look at the full creative process of how exactly we arrive at truly creative responses. Think of the process outlined below as one big funnel. You may come up with hundreds of ideas, decide that 20 are worth evaluating, three are worth testing, and one is worth implementing. We start with a lot of ideas, and funnel it down to one that we are really interested in.

This book focuses on the biggest part of the creative funnel, "Idea Brainstorming", but I still want you to understand the full creative process. Ideas alone are not enough. We need more than ideas to be successful in our creative ventures. Understanding the creative process in full will give you a head start to doing that.

1. **Idea Brainstorming** – coming up with ideas, for example, by using the idea hacks discussed in an upcoming section

2. **Idea Evaluation** – asking if those ideas are any good

3. **Preliminary Testing** – testing ideas in the real world, such as on people

4. **Implementing Ideas** – putting ideas into action on a larger scale

5. **Public reception and feedback** – does the public like it or not?

6. **Ongoing Improvements** – making changes based on feedback

This is just an overview. We will now go into the details of these processes.

Idea Brainstorming

This is the first part of the creative process. You will need to define what problem you are interested in. It can range from being very broad to very specific, which is up to you depending on your goals. For example, perhaps your broad goal is to write a novel. In that case, your ideas may start with figuring out the genre or the story type you want to go with. Later on, you may decide to get more and more specific, coming up with ideas for story lines, characters, heroes, villains, etc. The brainstorming process can be used for either broad or very specific problems. I would recommend getting specific if you can, but it is acceptable to start off with broad problems.

When you have your basic problem figured out, then you are ready to brainstorm. Your goal will be to come up with as many ideas as you possibly can, without questioning them at first. Your creativity will be facilitated when you allow the ideas to run like a stream. Stopping to question and evaluate them during this stage will ultimately slow you down. This can take a bit of practice for those of us who are used to evaluating everything, but it is an important thing to learn to do.

Early on when you are getting the hang of how to do this, I recommend repeated reminders to yourself that you are not evaluating these ideas right now, you are just forming them. With enough reminders, in time, you will not feel the need to automatically evaluate your ideas.

Evaluating Ideas

Your idea may be original, but is it practical?

Before starting the process of evaluation, make sure you have written down all of the ideas from your brainstorming session.

Afterwards, when ready to evaluate the ideas, you need to consider if they are practical. Will it cost too much in resources, time, or money to put the idea into action? Do you have access to any experts you will need for the project? Some ideas will cost you a large amount of money, but have a low chance to pay off in the way you would like. These ideas are probably not worth it. If you aren't sure how to evaluate an idea yourself, you will need to talk to experts or colleagues to help you with this.

As a side note, a concern of some creators is that they do not want to get help with their ideas because someone may steal them. Part of the solution to this problem is to work with people you trust. Find people who you are able to discuss ideas openly with, without fear that they will be stolen. Ideally, they should have their own successful ideas or work that they are preoccupied with.

The other thing to consider is that implementing an idea successfully is a lot of hard work. For example, it's silly to think that if I were to send the lyrics of a song to an average band, that they would produce a great song with it. And even if they did produce a masterpiece, in the end their song would probably be entirely different than the vision I actually had for it. The final creation is often very different from initial ideas. Keep in mind that although coming up with ideas takes work, actually creating something valuable takes a higher level of dedication.

A bigger problem for novice creators may actually be if they become too secretive with their work. It can be better to gain some feedback so as to improve, rather than to be completely closed off from the real world. Being overly secretive of your ideas will tend to stifle your creativity, since sharing and building ideas off of each other is a key way to be more creative.

What about gatekeepers and critical systems?

During your evaluation of your ideas, you have to "cross your t's and dot your i's" as they say, or you may regret it later. If there are any problems, holes, or likely setbacks with your idea, this is the time to figure it all out. Many of us, of course, will focus on evaluating the idea itself, but we also have to think about any other gatekeepers or critical systems involved. The gatekeepers are any judges who decide whether something is good enough to pass through or not. And critical systems are any processes such as a government or bureaucratic process of some kind that is necessary for you to pass through before you can proceed with implementing your idea.

No matter how good your idea is, if there is something stopping you from passing through the gatekeepers or any critical systems, you need to figure that out as soon as you can. It is possible there are difficult requirements you will need to resolve. Perhaps you will absolutely need a massive loan to have a chance to make your idea work, and you simply do not know how to get the money. Or what if there is a law in place that prevents you from using a certain material you absolutely need to move forward? Is there a bureaucratic process that will take years for you to get through, likely to make your creation obsolete by the time you implement it? In themselves, these are real problems to have to deal with. But imagine if you ignored it, and invested so much money, time, effort, and so forth creating something. Then at the end, you realized that there is this monster barrier in your path. It would be very unpleasant. You have to protect yourself against such a case by thinking ahead and figuring out how to handle the gatekeepers and critical systems early on.

Ultimately, you will have to decide how you deal with the gatekeepers and critical systems. You should consider meeting their requests, such as changing something about your creation or your process in order to speed up the process. Or you can be stubborn and fight against them, but realize that this could slow down your progress and you may not be able to move forward with your creation.

Preliminary Testing

By this point in the creative process you will have probably come up with many ideas, and narrowed down your focus to an original and useful idea. You've spent some time evaluating it, putting the idea through some level of scrutiny to make sure it is solid and that you can potentially be successful with implementing it.

This is a stage where depending on your field or your goals, you can take one of several related paths.

Create a Minimum viable product (MVP)

The minimum viable product (MVP) is when you create a product that is not in its final perfect state. Instead of getting everything the best that you possibly can, you are creating something that is in a "good enough" state to be used or experienced by whoever the intended audience is. Again, it does not necessarily need to be the best work. The purpose of the minimum viable product is to gauge whether further investments in time, money, and resources will be worthwhile.

For example, for the video game designer, a minimum viable product may involve a short video game with a few levels or stages and some basic graphics, rather than a long and incredibly elaborate game with the best graphics. Video games can take a long while to design anyway, but perhaps it is better to dedicate several months to a MVP than it is to dedicate several years to an overly-elaborate project and then find that there were key flaws or there just wasn't as much interest in your creation as you would have hoped.

The above example is meant to illustrate that forming an MVP helps to avoid the disaster of over-investing in an idea destined to fail. In any field, if one MVP fails, you can simply move on to creating another one, until you find something that appears to work. When you create an MVP that is performing well, you can invest in fleshing out that idea and making it bigger or more elaborate, to satisfy your audience. The MVP is an effective way to create things which are more likely to succeed in an efficient way.

Build a prototype

The prototype is simply another way of looking at the MVP. The MVP is usually focused on creating something that is viable for the customer. During this phase, you may have questions such as "Can the customer use this product and give me some reliable feedback?" Whereas with a prototype, the focus tends to be more on questions such as "Is this something that I can get to work in the real world?" Traditionally, inventors who are creating something new, and are not certain if their ideas are feasible, will refer to prototypes. Business people are more likely to refer to MVPs. However, there aren't strict limits as to when these concepts can be used.

Prototypes will involve their own special challenges because the basic idea of a prototype typically involves creating something smaller than it will be in its final size. For example, if you had a new type of solar panel you wanted to create, to put on homes, instead of building massive panels for homes first, it would be more practical to create a smaller version. Then you could see if that prototype works effectively, given its size. This may work well for solar panels, but certain creations will be difficult to test without making it at its final expected size. For example, it might not make much sense to build a smaller prototype of a rocket ship and try to get it to the moon. The physics and challenges involved would be different enough that working on a prototype may not be worth it. Also, the costs involved may be around just as high, making this completely impractical.

Making a prototype still makes sense in a variety of circumstances. If you have the attention of investors, but they need more evidence that your idea can truly work, a prototype will be useful. If you are seeking a patent to have full ownership of your idea, a prototype will also be helpful. As said above, if you are uncertain if your idea can even work, and to come up with the capital to make the final creation would be ridiculously high, building a prototype could be a good idea. Also, if it is relatively easy and convenient to build a prototype, in comparison to building your final product, it could be a good idea to do so. The point when you have to reconsider whether building a prototype is worth it is when it will cost you immensely to create it. In that case, you might decide to just build your final product and take a risk on it.

Get feedback

Many people, when thinking of being creative, probably do not have feedback in mind. It appears so uncreative, to sit around asking people what they think of your work. But this is actually important. Creativity confuses many people, because we tend to hear about lone creative geniuses who make brilliant discoveries. But in reality, creativity happens in part from time spent alone thinking, and in part from time spent sharing and exchanging ideas. Having both in the process will tend to allow for the most creative ideas. To get this concept across, think of how you would want your personal home designed. It's possible you would like some interesting and unusual things. Maybe you would want a bar built into your kitchen. Maybe you would want a glass ceiling in your room to see the natural light. Maybe you would want one of your rooms to function as a greenhouse for your plants. These are all interesting ideas, and consider if you personally wanted them. Of course, the reason feedback is important is that just because something appeals to you doesn't mean anyone else would be interested in it. You may be in for an unpleasant shock when you find you can't sell the home because no one else appreciated the style.

Exchanging ideas with others and understanding what people want and need is a central part of the creative process. Think of who judges creative works for what they are. It isn't a single individual, usually. There may be some big influencers, but in the end, it is the public that decides what is creative. If they decide your creation is either unoriginal or not useful, then your creation will go unappreciated. In such a circumstance, you have several options. You may simply accept this and move on to another idea, you may try to make them understand the value of your creation, or you may make modifications to your ideas so that they have more appeal to the masses.

I hope you understand that during your "preliminary testing" phase, you will want to get some feedback to help make sure you are making creative progress. Now, let's consider some of the different ways you can get feedback on your creative work.

You can get feedback from other experts in your field. If you can find some of them who are willing to help assess your creation, this could be very useful. Experts will understand the problems in your industry and probably have a unique perspective and ability to give helpful feedback. Something to consider is that the more original your idea is, going against expected conventions in your area, the less likely it is for even an expert to be supportive. This may happen, and you will need to be the final judge as to whether their comments reflect true problems in your creation, or whether they are biased against what you have made simply because it is new and different.

Of course, the other place to go for feedback is your own audience – if you already have one, or if not, you can search for the type of people who are likely to want your creation. They will mostly be interested in whether the product meets their needs and wants. If it does not, they will not be happy, no matter how original your idea was. If you plan to charge for your business or services, you will want to pay special attention to whether your main audience is willing to pay for your creation. People naturally want to be nice, usually, so be cautious of assuming their optimism is a sign that your product will do well in the marketplace. You may ask them directly what they would be willing to pay for it, and follow up asking if they would like to pre-order the product. This will help you see if they are truly serious about spending money on your product. Then, you can record any contact information of theirs and get back to them when you have your final product or service ready.

When taking the feedback you get into account, you need to be confident in accepting the role of final decision-maker. You don't necessarily need to apply all of the feedback you get. Primarily, you will want to consider the feedback on whether it is useful and on its practicality. Usefulness is whether the idea would improve your product and make it better in some way. Practicality is whether you can achieve those improvements in a reasonable time and cost, and whether the benefits you get will be worth those costs. Ultimately, those decisions are up to you. Even experts can have conflicting opinions with each other. And of course, some of your audience may prefer things one way, and other members may prefer it another way.

Implementing Ideas

Unfortunately, even if you have had good ideas, evaluated them, and received useful feedback, it is no guarantee that you will be able to successfully implement them. Sometimes, everything looks good on paper but then it doesn't go as expected in practice. Nonetheless, you stand the best chance to succeed with your ideas by going through the full creative process rather than skipping steps.

Implementing your ideas successfully is often not easy. You may want help from others to do this. Possibly, you will need to hire workers or consultants or have other experts help in some way. You may find that you still have much to learn before you can put your ideas into action. Some of your time may be spent learning about what materials you will need, techniques, processes involved, researching the market, and figuring out the specifics of how you will provide your service or create your product.

Ideally, you would be an expert in your area, but to actually apply your idea may require expertise in different areas, such as marketing, engineering, customer service, and so forth. Perhaps you are only an expert in one or two of the areas you need. In that case, you will need to do extensive learning fast, or you will need extra help on those areas in which you are weak.

Public Reception

If you have made it this far in the creative process, you are doing very well. This is the sort of "moment of truth" as to how your idea will ultimately do. You have evaluated it, tested it, and implemented it. Now, you have to observe how the public reacts.

Have you created something original and useful that the public is interested in? Were you able to find your target audience? Keep in mind that a lack of results at this point might not mean your idea was bad. It could just mean you need to execute it better. For example, perhaps you didn't do enough to inform, via marketing, your audience that your product or service even exists. In a world with services such as eBay which make it easy for anyone to create and sell, you have to consider the reality of a crowded marketplace.

Ask yourself, have you done everything possible to truly make your creation stand out? Does it offer a better solution than the competition? Is it available at a competitive price, making it more likely to sell? Is your presentation of it polished? For example, have you used colors that go well together and are appealing to your audience – this can apply for both your product and any marketing materials you use.

You can still run into problems even at this later stage in the creative process, but if you believe in your idea and creation, and you have gone thoroughly through all of the creative steps above, this is not the time to give up.

Nonetheless, as they say, "you only get one chance to make a first impression". If you can launch your creation in the best possible way, this will help you gain momentum, rather than realizing along the way that you made mistake after mistake. You want those first customers, clients, or viewers to be thrilled by your creation and to spread the word, not to go on to the next thing and forget about what you did. This is why going through all of the creative steps is so important.

Ongoing Improvements & Checking for Problems

Rather than simply telling you that creativity is a tough thing to be successful at, I hoped to show you this in all of these creative steps. When you have made your creation, even if it is successful and you have many people interested and checking it out, and they love it and spread the word, your work isn't quite done yet.

Even major multi-million dollar companies can go bankrupt. The ideas that you come up with will be very important in your creative endeavors, but ultimately, everything you do with that idea, such as evaluating it and implementing it will also play a big role in making it a success. After this, you will also want to keep making ongoing improvements and continue to check for problems, to have the best chance at success.

Most people, when they think of improvements will think that they need to improve the same product or service, over and over. This is often what the goal is, but if for some reason you decide you would like to move on to another creative goal, you can still make improvements in this new area based on what you learned in your older creative projects. Either you make improvements to your current project, or you take what you've learned from that project and apply it to a whole new other project. Carrying the learning to new projects is what serial inventors and entrepreneurs do to have great creative success.

You may not think of this stage as part of the creative process, but it is, because any creation that ignores this step is much more likely to fail. Ultimately, the goal will be to succeed with your creations, in which case you will want to include this step. As an example, even the greatest artwork needs to be checked for problems. In time, a sculpture may crack. The color on a painting may fade. Paintings will need specific kinds of lighting in order to avoid degrading too quickly. These are all things that need to be maintained to keep the creation at its top level of quality. To ignore these needs would mean the destruction of the original work. As you can see, we must avoid such outcomes in our own projects.

The Bad News: We are Losing Our Creativity

Schools Cut Creative Programs

"My contention is that creativity now is as important in education as
literacy, and we should treat it with the same status"

– Sir Ken Robinson, International advisor on education in the arts to
government, non-profits, education and arts bodies

I've read on many occasions about schools cutting arts, music, and recess – in sources such as the Washington Times, US News, Forbes,
NPR, and many other outlets. Such funding cuts often happen because
a school is faced with needing to remove an expense in order to stay
within their budget. To meet their goal, they tend to see the arts as areas that they can remove while still maintaining a learning facility. Unfortunately, there are costs for such actions.

It's true that children can learn in school without art, music, and recess.
But when you spend your whole day learning what you are instructed
on, with little room for your own spontaneous creations, creativity suf-
fers. Perhaps it will take some creative thinking from administrators to
gather funds or to make a path to help children be creative again.

Unfortunately, these school budget cuts may play a role in reducing the
creativity of children. Sir Ken Robinson, chair of the UK Government's report on creativity, education, and the economy has described
the research as such:

> Of 1,600 children aged three to five who were tested, 98% showed they could
> think in divergent ways. By the time they were aged eight to 10, 32% could
> think divergently. When the same test was applied to 13 to 15-year-olds, only
> 10% could think in this way. And when the test was used with 200,000 25-
> year-olds, only 2% could think divergently. (TESS, 25 March 2005)

Thinking divergently, or the ability to come up with many different ideas or solutions, is a significant part of the creative process. The above research findings have clearly shown that as children age they tend to become less and less creative. Ultimately, those with the least creative potential tend to be adults. Of course, there is something we can do about that, to reawaken our natural creativity. We will cover that shortly.

We Consume Much More Than We Produce

In the "old days", people didn't have TVs and smartphones. They often had to create their own games or entertainment to pass the time. Now, we have widespread and mass production to cover every possible need someone could have. For example, there appear to be hundreds of brands of toothpaste to choose from. With such an easy selection – for virtually all kinds of products, not just toothpaste – we lose the motivation to create things for ourselves. Humans going back even a few generations, however, were more creative out of necessity. They may have made their own clothing, toothpaste, soap, and elected to fix anything that broke instead of replacing it.

Consuming creative products doesn't necessarily make us less creative, though. But we spend much of our time using the creations of others and accepting them, rather than questioning them and proposing our own alternatives. Rather than invest in our own creativity, we tend to complain about the products we are unhappy with. If enough people are unsatisfied, either the original company will find a way to fix the problem for the unsatisfied customers, or a new company will create a better solution. Of course, in many cases, companies are able to efficiently make their creations, and we are more than willing to pay the price to save time. It is convenient, but we tend to do this with practically everything. We acquire the habit of waiting for solutions from big companies, rather than to seek them out on our own.

Many of us today are exercising the opposite of self-reliance. We rely on ourselves in the sense that we have jobs and earn income. But we rely on countless others in the sense that we spend this money to have others find creative solutions for us. If someone is using an ineffective medicine, they expect researchers to create a new and better one. If we are unsatisfied with a smartphone, we expect the competition to create a better one. Of course, often this approach makes sense, as the big companies have the knowledge and capital to arrive at effective solutions rather quickly. But the point is we become used to a lifestyle of relying on big businesses and big money to be creative for us. We stop seeing ourselves as someone who can create anything meaningful, which is not the case.

To illustrate the pitfalls of this, imagine if all the young people today lacked any interest in how things worked. All they did was use smart phones and computers, but everyone forgot how these things actually functioned and how to make better ones. In time, we would stop having anyone around who actually knew how to create them or fix them. Eventually, all the existing ones would break and all further generations would be at a loss. This is an extreme example, but it shows that we absolutely need to keep our creativity alive, understanding how things work, and how to improve them, to always build up on the past creatives accomplishments, or risk regressions that set us back as a species.

There is a bit of a paradox here. I'm discussing how we are losing our creativity, but at the same time I am also saying that big creative businesses are ready to step in and solve our creative problems. Big businesses are in a sense, paid to be creative, paid to have the solutions to the problems us consumers have. The paradox is that the more creative big businesses are in solving problems, the less creative the mass population feels it needs to be, in their personal lives. The thinking will be that the important things are already being handled. They can live their own quiet lives and binge watch the new hot series on TV while someone else creates the solutions to their problems.

So, it seems humans are still very creative, but it appears that the creativity of the species is concentrated mostly into the small groups of people who are paid to create. These are the people who work for the big corporations that solve problems.

But why leave all the fun to those creatives? A corporation works on finding general creative solutions for the masses, not for your personal problems. Relying on big businesses may work for your general problems, but not do much for you in your unique daily problems. You are the one who needs to get creative and tackle those, as no one else has the motivation or understanding of the problems to take care of it.

The benefit of bringing back this personal level of creativity in our lives would be that we could become healthier by creating our own organic products to consume, more self-sufficient and resourceful, and we could also gain the ability to make things that are more customizable to our specific needs, rather than "a one size fits all" product. Another benefit is that there is a unique enjoyment that comes from entertaining yourself rather than always using products or screens to do so.

We are Encouraged to Function on Autopilot, as Automatons, not Creators

In the workplace, and also in society in general, what is tested and proven to work is highly valued. This is obvious, since it helps with efficiency. Workers end up getting more done in less time, which makes the boss happy. Although, keep in mind that what appears to be efficient now can be proven inefficient in the years to come, probably by a creative person who discovers that something different works even better than the way things are usually done.

In many modern work environments, people are motivated to apply the most efficient systems that they can, rather than a creative one. This becomes the benchmark for how to do a task, and everyone follows in line to do the same task in the same way. Again, rather than aspire to be creative ourselves, we will tend to rely on the few creative individuals to possibly make a breakthrough. Many of us will be uninterested or unwilling to take a risk and do something creative. And perhaps that is reasonable, if you work in an environment where creativity is discouraged and can actually get you fired. But there is another cost to this. This autopilot thinking will drain our creativity as time passes. The less we exercise our creative abilities, the more they will tend to fade away.

Even though creativity is important, you should also be aware that there are risks to being creative in the workplace. Your superiors may see creative activity as a risk, or a threat to getting things done efficiently. A new creative idea can threaten leadership structures. For example, if an entry-level worker has a great creative idea that makes a massive improvement in the organization, then should he be promoted over others in leadership positions? Possibly, but that outcome seems very unlikely. Creative ideas are likely to call into question other more established and respected ways of doing things, which will threaten anyone who created those systems or those who have come to rely on them. You can count on the people who are used to the old way to resist a new and unproven way of doing things. Perhaps they aren't so concerned with your new idea, as they are that the idea will disrupt everything they are used to and threaten their personal status.

Creativity is a good thing, we just need to consider what the reactions of others may be to our creative ideas. If they will be positive, you can share your ideas. If they will be negative, it may be best to wait for a better time to share them. Understand that in a typical organization, the priority is placed on getting the best results. If you can prove or demonstrate that your new creative approach gets better results, you will be more likely to succeed in convincing your superiors that your idea is worth implementing.

We are Too Quick to Look up Answers

I believe it is an excellent idea to read and learn anything we wish. And a part of learning is to look up answers to questions you might have. However, we sometimes look up answers too quickly. For many questions, even direct factual questions like "How tall is Mount Everest?" I think it could be useful to turn it into a creative exercise of coming up with possible answers, and reasons why those answers may be correct. Perhaps you know how tall the Eiffel tower is, or the average skyscraper, or something else. Then perhaps you can create your own ballpark answer. After you have used your creativity to come up with a possible solution, you may look up what the true answer is.

For creative problems, I believe we should first do a mental search of possible solutions. When you need ideas to solve such a problem, I think you are better off exercising your own creative abilities to come up with a list of your own responses, instead of simply Googling it. Search engines can help us with gathering facts, but using them to generate creative solutions for us will only do our personal creativity a disservice. In time, we are likely to lose our ability to create much, if we always rely on search engines to give us ideas.

Personally, I avoid using Google to search for creative solutions for another reason. I find that after I have access to a large list of Google solutions, it becomes harder to think outside of the scope of what the search engine is telling me. When the search findings lead me to think in certain directions, my mind automatically gets stuck in that frame of mind, and I may be less likely to come up with more original and creative solutions which go in a different direction.

For example, if I were trying to think up animals, and I find a huge list of animals online, and it goes "dog, cat, gerbil, hamster, parakeet..." then my mind will probably get stuck in thinking of house pets. I may be less likely to come up with animals that rarely live in the house, like "bat, lion, zebra, elephant, crocodile," etc. Of course, this is problematic for creativity, as the goal is to *not* get locked into one way of thinking. If I do want to use Google as an aide, then I come up with my own ideas first, and then I check it against the search engine results.

Another problem is I often feel my creative energy is drained by the common long lists of answers found online. It is typical to find a list of a hundred ways to solve a given problem. The issue with this is it can be time-consuming and sometimes exhausting thinking about all of those solutions, which leaves little energy to come up with my own ideas.

I have to admit that there is a huge authoritative aura to Google. To its credit, Google continues to improve its system, becoming even more and more of an authority. For example, if you search for specific information or answers, you will frequently get one response that is the best and is summarized at the top of your search results. You don't even need to click on anything, the answer just pops up right in front of you. This is very low effort and you immediately get answers to your questions. It's simple, easy, and fast, but it's *too easy*. You don't even have to think of any possibilities. The answer is just there. Unfortunately, since we train ourselves to stop thinking and just accept the authority, we rarely question the answers given. You might think, "If it's good enough for Google, its good enough for me." But again, this restricts our creative potential, for we stop looking for better solutions. We assume the Google solution is the best we'll ever get, which is true… until one person gets creative and proves this to be wrong.

Of course, I use Google, and I think it is a wonderful and powerful tool. My issue here is not with Google itself, but with the fact that we need to adjust to the technology as fast as it is also adjusting and improving. We need to use these tools to help our minds become stronger and more resilient, not weaker, and over-reliant upon them. Keep using Google. I use it too. But don't allow it – or any other tool – to restrict your creative potential.

As an example of how we can become over-reliant on technology, consider the calculator. It has been a wonderful tool, saving us time on mental calculations. However, I recall being in school surrounded by students who lost the ability to perform simple math operations in their heads. They relied so heavily on a calculator that they couldn't do math without it. In many cases, they may have forgotten how to do the operations by hand, especially in the case of long-form multiplication and division. The thesaurus is another example of a good tool, but the price has been our ability to think of similar words without it. The problem is that over-reliance on too many tools will restrict our own creative abilities if we do not use some of our energy to generate our own solutions first.

I believe I have explained this issue thoroughly now, and I am sure you are ready to move on. But the reason for this elaboration of how we are too quick to look up answers is because I believe this issue is highly relevant in the modern world, and this is something that will not be going away any time soon.

The Good News: We Are More Creative Than We Think We Are

It's in Our Species, in Our Genes

I want to give a brief overview here of a small sampling of some of the creations of humanity, going in order from the distant past up to the present day. This is to show you that we have an extensive creative history as a species.

2.6 million years ago – Stone tools

1 million years ago – Discovered fire

170 thousand years ago – Clothing

100 thousand years ago – Human burial sites

40 thousand years ago – Cave paintings

30 thousand years ago – Domestication of dogs

28 thousand years ago – Rope

13 thousand years ago - Agriculture

8,000 BCE – Proto-city – large permanent settlements

3,500 BCE – Domestication of horses

3,500 BCE – The wheel

3,000 BCE – Writing

2,600 BCE – Pyramids built

1,700 BCE – The alphabet

400 BCE – Mirror

9th century – Gunpowder

13th century – Soap

1440 – Printing press

1798 – Smallpox vaccine

1804 - Full-scale working railway steam locomotive (train)

1876 – Telephone

1879 – Practical lightbulb

1885 – Automobile

1903 – Successful flight

1915 – Military tank

1927 – Television

1946 – Digital computer

1968 – Virtual reality system

1969 – Humans land on the moon

1970 – Pocket calculator

1971 – Personal computer

1971 – Email

1983 –3D printer

1989 – Worldwide web (the internet)

1994 – Amazon.com, Inc. is launched

1997 – Artificial intelligence system (Deep Blue) beats world chess champion (Garry Kasparov) in a tournament matchup

1997 – Mars land rover lands on Mars

2004 – Facebook

2005 – YouTube

2007 – iPhone

2011 – IBM Watson (an artificially intelligent computer)

2012 – Google driverless car

2022+ – SpaceX plans to send humans to Mars

Why Are We Such a Creative Species?

I think this is an obvious question you might have when we see just how many creations we have gone through, and the fact that this is really the tiniest sample possible of our creative history. There have been many, many creations, some minor, and some so influential they have changed the way humans lived forever afterward.

It is tough to answer why our ancestors were creative, but I have some ideas as to why this was the case. And if you have ever read an article on what makes humans intelligent, or what separates us in ability from other animals, the answers are somewhat similar.

First, consider the human brain. The natural evolution of the human brain has helped us to become more creative than other animals. The ability to plan, visualize, and simulate events in the mind all play their role in our creative ability. It is likely that we developed such abilities earlier on in our evolution as a way to aid in our survival. Although I will not go into detail here on the exact neuroscience, I believe it is clear that the evolved human brain has provided us with the basic ability to be creative.

Second, we have vocal chords. This ability to speak (of course the brain helps with this) is hugely important because we can share ideas easily. And sharing and mixing ideas together in interesting ways plays a big role in creativity. We are also able to give each other specific feedback and improve on our creations even more. If we could not discuss our creative ideas, it would be highly frustrating. Many creative projects involve multiple people, and of course those people need to share ideas or the creative process will stall.

Third, the way our hands are built helps us to manipulate objects. And of course, to make many of our ideas a reality, we need to manipulate objects. Think of how important the hands are for making things happen in the real world. It is actually possible that we could be highly creative without having hands, but it would be a very frustrating existence. We would perhaps have incredibly vivid imaginations and concoct interesting stories in our minds, and come up with all sorts of possibilities on how to solve problems, but on a practical level it would be very difficult to make any of this happen in the real world.

Fourth, if we look at more modern human times, the invention of Gutenberg's printing press (in 1440) made information much more freely available. You need a basic amount of information to be able to create something meaningful, so this was a big breakthrough. Information could travel in the form of a book from place to place. A big benefit was also that you no longer needed a living person to tell you his or her ideas. A person who had died could still communicate, through the writing which lived on in a printed book. Actually, books had existed before this, so all of this was already possible. But the printing press accelerated this process so that multiple books could be printed relatively quickly and distributed to even more people.

Fifth, let's lump together computers (or any smartphones or devices that use the internet), and the internet itself. The internet has resulted in an information boom, where there is so much content available that even going through a fraction of it would not be possible in a lifetime. We now have easy access to books, reports, articles, tools, instructional videos, and other resources to help learn virtually anything. Also, people from around the world are able to communicate with each other, spreading and sharing ideas at the click of a button. This worldwide network allows not only a great access to information, but the ability for people to connect this information in new ways to help form creative solutions.

Sixth, are initiatives to expand the internet to actually be worldwide. Despite the common nickname of the internet, the "worldwide web", around two out of three people around the world do not have access to it. Many companies and organizations are working to change this, in what has been described as the Internet Space Race.

Google Loon is sending balloons to outer space to increase internet coverage. Internet.org (Facebook) is sending out drones to provide access to the internet. And SpaceX will be launching satellites to provide such coverage as well. With such organizations competing to bring worldwide internet coverage at a lower cost, it seems inevitable that most people around the world will soon have access to the largest source of information. Of course, information itself doesn't cause creativity, but being exposed to information and other peoples' ideas is a great first step to getting creative. Without it, meaningful creative solutions become unlikely as one becomes isolated from the progress being made in the rest of the world.

Seventh, and this hasn't happened yet, but the next frontier for expanding the creativity of the species will likely involve creativity nootropics (or mind-enhancing drugs), or it may involve brain chip implants that expand our creative abilities. I believe such advancements are more likely to happen with intelligence before we see them with creativity, however. For now, this will have to remain the stuff of science fiction.

Dreams are Proof of our Natural Creativity

We all dream, which takes a lot of creative energy. Dreams appear to occur in real time, meaning that in your dreams, everything happens immediately. You do not write up a script for how your dream is going to go before you go to bed, and then dream out what you scripted in the night. The dream appears to simultaneously be scripted and executed. Let's take a moment to think of everything involved in an average dream. In my dreams, there is typically an environment, as in real life. I could be inside a home, on the streets in a car, in a park, the wilderness, etc. As in real life, I may be alone, or I may be surrounded by a few people, or a huge group. Often, there is some kind of a story or drama taking place. Someone is being attacked, I'm looking for someone or something that I desperately need, or I may be at a gathering with friends, to name a few scenarios.

This is all interesting to me, because in my waking life, it is rather difficult to keep up with so many different things happening all at once. Can you keep up with paying attention to the background scenery, everyone in a room, all the discussions and activities happening, and any thoughts you may be also having, all at the same time? I cannot, but possibly you can. If you can though, can you then simulate and create all of this in your mind, in real time? Again, this means you cannot stop and think what conversations or actions will take place, or what you will do in the dream. It all needs to happen smoothly, without pauses. At this point you will probably tell me you cannot do that, I suspect. And my response will be, "Yes you can." You do it every night in your sleep, of course. In our sleep, much of our brain power automatically gets used in these dreams, but in waking life we need our mental energy for other things like planning the day and executing our plans, not in a wildly imaginative process.

We are creative every day, or rather, every night. If you need a reminder of this, write down your dreams first thing in the morning. As an added bonus, your dreams may spark your creativity because they tend to be the workings of the subconscious and flow in various directions, unrestricted by the limitations of the real world.

As Children, We Show High Creative Potential

It may be hard to remember this far back, but as children it is likely that many of us drove our parents wild with our imaginations. Children are known to have imaginary friends, the desire to pretend to be cowboys or princesses, and sometimes make stories up for the fun of it.

I actually have a memory of being a child myself, and still being surprised at the endless creative energy of another *younger* child. I was around 10, and my parents left me to play with a girl that was probably around six. I remember getting annoyed quickly because every phrase that came out of her mouth was "Let's pretend that..." By 10 years old, I no longer related to the imaginary world she was constantly creating, although I may have if I were also six. My mother's friend told me not to get so annoyed, because I was exactly the same at her age. I believe this sort of need to pretend, imagine, and create is common in those younger years. This is something many of us will lose as we get older, or the way we create will simply change for others.

Our ability to create things as children is naturally quite high. However, children are not fully creative, technically, and this is because to be creative we need to essentially intermix the adult and child ways of thinking. Children are original, creating their imaginary lives, creatures, and making things up with ease. Adults are very orderly, looking for high quality solutions and not necessarily concerned if they are new or original. As established earlier, truly creative solutions have both originality and quality. Children are set up to be highly creative (mostly original), but they are not experienced enough in anything yet to judge and evaluate and form high quality solutions. Originality tends to be easy for children and difficult for adults. Whereas adults are often experienced enough to judge high quality solutions well, and children lack that experience and tend to not realize the difference between good or poor quality solutions.

If you need to be convinced that you are at all creative, think of your childhood. Did you play games like house, war, cowboys and robbers, or something else? Did you pretend or imagine wild things? Did you draw? It can be tough to remember, but try. I am sure you did do some sort of creative activity that perhaps you have lost touch with in time. Remembering these things will allow you to see that we all have some natural creativity in us. The goal then may not be a matter of getting creative, but learning how to be creative as we once were, or to reawaken our creativity.

Simple Yet Highly Effective Tips to Be More Creative

Tip #1: Deal with a Fear of Rejection

There is something that stops many of us from being creative, actually it stops us before we even start. This is fear. Many of us want to be liked and accepted by others. To be criticized doesn't feel good, so clearly most of us prefer to fit in the best way that we can. However, a big part of creating something, even creating ideas, is to eventually put them out there for people to judge. Therefore, the person who creates will always have something in the public eye. And people will be there to critique, some positive assessments, and of course, some negative. We tend to fear those negative reactions, which makes it difficult to get started.

Maybe this isn't a problem for you, but I must discuss it here because I am aware this is a big obstacle for many people.

One way to get around this fear is to shield yourself from such criticisms. I don't recommend this strategy in the long-term, because I think it is best to learn to overcome fears rather than to avoid them. However, the tip here is *not* to mention your creative projects to anyone early on. When you are just coming up with rough ideas, you may feel hurt if you mention it to someone and they poke holes and identify big problems immediately. You may doubt yourself and feel bad about it, demotivating you to continue. Instead, spend more time on your project, elaborating it, researching it, fleshing out ideas, eliminating the ones that aren't so good, and thinking of likely critiques. Do all of this before you mention your ideas publically.

In the short term, you may avoid criticisms, but in the long-term I recommend overcoming this fear. You have to welcome criticisms because these will help you advance in your work. You will need some encouragement to keep moving forward, but you also need some negative feedback to help you improve your ideas. Something that helps me is to always remember that criticisms are actually good. Ultimately, they will help you make a better product or service, and to improve in what you do.

Even if it turns out you had a bad idea and went in the wrong direction, remember that you can always get more ideas. And even if a critic rejects your idea, this doesn't necessarily mean it is bad. Possibly, the person assessing it is wrong, or you simply need to make some changes to improve your idea. An upcoming section on idea hacks will show you how to always come up with new ideas, so if one fails it is not a big problem for you. This in itself should reduce your fear of rejections or even failures.

Tip #2: Learn New Things in Broad Areas, Regularly, through Different Channels

What will help your creativity is exposing yourself to new things. You will find it helpful to say yes to new opportunities that come your way more often than not. The important thing is not to automatically shut off something new. Before you say "No" to something, ask what you have to lose and what you might have to gain. Sometimes, you may feel unprepared for something new, but ask yourself if there are really any downsides to simply trying. Perhaps you will learn something new or be thrilled in a way you never had been. These new experiences end up being more raw material for us to use in our creative ideas. Every new thing you see and experience is a chance to spark more ideas.

You will also find it helpful to read widely, in many different areas. Sometimes, you will learn something and then find that you can apply it to an area that seems completely unrelated. I would recommend reading from different books, news outlets, magazines, and so forth. Some other ways to get new ideas are to watch foreign movies, travel, or listen to a wide range of music, including from international sources. As you can see, generally opening yourself up to new experiences will be good for your ability to generate new ideas.

Tip #3: Make No Excuses

When you do get stuck, don't simply tell yourself "I can't think of anything, so I better do something else". Part of being successful with coming up with ideas is to persist. You should strain a bit and push past the initial desire to give up. There will be times when the ideas flow easily, and other times they may not. When they are not flowing easily, be prepared to work a little bit more.

When you have trouble coming up with ideas and you give up fast, you train yourself to think you are not creative. This will lead you to think that you cannot come up with anything and that you are mentally blocked. This isn't the right way to go. If you persist just a little bit longer, you will likely find that you are creative and form plenty of new ideas.

In my experience, the first idea can be the toughest to come up with. After that, they tend to flow out like water. One interesting idea can quickly lead to another, and another, and another, like a chain reaction. Eventually the ideas will bubble out of you into one big explosion. But none of this happens if you give up after a minute or two.

I recommend setting a timer for 10 minutes when you want to generate ideas. Make the goal to either come up with 100 ideas or to come up with as many ideas as possible in 10 minutes. After the 10 minutes are up or you have your 100 ideas, you are done. Through all that time, stay in your seat (or at least your room), stay focused, and don't allow your mind to wander to thinking that you are blocked and can't come up with anything. Stay focused on the task.

This may sound tough right now, and painful to commit to even 10 minutes of coming up with new ideas. What if you can't even come up with one idea in 10 minutes? Well, then start another 10 minute session. This is very important. You have to train yourself to understand that you are creative. Keep starting new sessions until you get at least one idea. It doesn't have to be the best idea ever. It doesn't necessarily even have to be original or a quality idea, it just needs to be an idea.

You may be thinking that many ideas are not necessarily creative. If it doesn't have originality or quality, then it lacks creativity. And you would be correct, but the phase of creativity where we come up with ideas is about coming up with more and more ideas. Evaluating it for originality and quality, and whether it is truly creative is a different stage. To mix up these stages will slow you down, and make you second guess every idea you have. Therefore, you should train yourself to think in a manner where you have no filter whatsoever, at least for short periods while you are coming up with ideas. This may take practice, but you can learn it. Every time you start evaluating while you are coming up with ideas, stop yourself, and remember that evaluating and judging the ideas is for another stage.

Tip #4: Come up with One New Idea, Every Day

I know this contradicts the above section where I recommend being very persistent. But depending on your creative background and your natural rhythms, this approach may work better. You can try both and see what you think. If you feel overwhelmed with trying to be creative, or just completely blocked, or unmotivated to get started, this can be a better system to start up your creativity again. Or clearly, if putting pressure on yourself to come up with ideas on a 10 minute timer simply isn't working for you, I recommend trying this instead. Either way can be useful. Try both ways and see what works for you.

With this system, you will come up with one idea per day on anything that is important to you. Perhaps you need ideas for your next painting. Then you can come up with ideas for that. Or we can go deeper. A novelist may already know his basic book idea, but perhaps he needs ideas for more characters. His goal could be to come up with a new character idea every day. A business person may need new creative marketing ideas. If you are working on multiple creative projects, you may decide to come up with one new idea for all of those projects, per day.

What you may think is that you want to get creative. One idea per day won't do much for your progress. I understand this thinking, and I would probably think the same thing too if it weren't for my own experience using this method. When I used this system, I committed to coming up with two ideas per day, one idea in different areas. One is in nonfiction book ideas, the other was in business improvement ideas – such as marketing. It started off slow, but as the weeks went on of persisting with this system, I was coming up with more and more ideas, seemingly without effort. At first, I had to try to come up with them, but after a while, they just flooded out of me, uncontrollable at times. At my peak, I was sometimes coming up with over a hundred ideas in a day. The key here is that this was without meaning to. I didn't sit down and try to do it, it just happened. The habit of coming up with two simple ideas per day essentially built a habit, where my mind was always trying to come up with more and more ideas, whether I consciously made the effort or not.

The ironic thing is coming up with too many ideas can be a distraction. After a certain period I backed off from generating so many ideas because I needed to use more of my time on executing them. Nonetheless, it's great to have systems like this in your toolkit to come up with new ideas whenever you need them.

I originally got the idea for this system with James Altucher. He recommends coming up with 10 ideas per day in his blog article, "The Ultimate Guide for Becoming an Idea Machine". But I found such great results from coming up with very few ideas per day that I never found it necessary to make 10 the goal.

Tip #5: Change up Your Schedule, Routines, Habits, Etc.

Your environment, or the scenery around you can make a difference as to how motivated you feel to create. Fortunately, you have the ability to influence where you go, and the environment you will therefore see, at least to some extent. For example, perhaps you can leave your home and go outside, or visit a nearby park. Going to another country may be too far to be practical, but you can still move around to help break the monotony and start feeling more creative.

If you are staring at a blank word processor on your computer screen and unable to come up with any ideas, after a while it makes sense to change the scenery. You could see if moving and doing something else can help spark some new ideas. When you are feeling drained and burnt out, rather than continuing to press yourself onward after a certain point, it makes sense to take a break. You will likely find it helpful to relax and get your mind off work and then watch some TV or take a nap.

Instead of spending all day inside, get out and get some fresh air or sunshine, get some exercise, or meet someone new. Try picking up a random book off of the library shelf. Experiment with a new exercise. Meditate. Write a book. See what kind of painting you can create. Freestyle some new music on the piano (or a piano app). Learn some new words and phrases in a foreign language. Do something different.

If you are overflowing with ideas as it is, then you are fine. But when you are blocked, you need to be open to changing things up. The mind can grow stale from being in the same room all day, around the same people, doing the same things at the same time.

Personally, I have many routines in my life, but routines can be good for increasing work efficiency. However, I make sure to mix things up by traveling regularly. Also, I read widely in many different areas, which helps me connect new ideas.

Tip #6: Figure out What Area You Want to Be Creative In

What is the one thing you want to be creative in? If you don't know, your key goal should be to figure this out. But if you have no idea, there is no need to worry. This is the time to really let loose and have fun. You can try a variety of creative tasks and see what you think. Or you can take something you are already good at, and think of how you can bring creativity into it.

Think about what your main goals are. For example, do you want to come up with new ideas for a startup business, or ideas for new graphic designs, or new ideas for how to landscape your backyard? Whatever it is, if it is important, then work on that area daily. In doing so, your abilities will improve drastically the longer you apply yourself to it.

When you know what area you want to be creative in, you can then begin to focus your energy on that. Or if you prefer, you can work on different creative areas, but your progress may come more slowly. Often, to be truly creative you will want to build up some expertise in an area. So to be creative in physics versus writing versus architecture will involve completely unique sets of problems. And of course, building up your expertise will take time, separate from your endeavors to generate new ideas. To start off, I would recommend focusing on one creative area at a time. You don't necessarily need to be a full expert, but it will be important to be well informed and to build up experience in the area you wish to be creative.

Tip #7: The #1 Habit of the Most Creative Individuals (You've been doing it since you were one year old)

The #1 habit that gets my creative juices flowing, and which has also worked for countless highly creative people, is something most of us can do from the age of one. It's simply walking. I walk as part of my routine almost every day, and this is the part of my day where I have consistently had the most ideas. In time, through consistency with the habit, my ideas have overall become higher and higher in quality. I have been lucky because I currently live near a beach. I often get to see the sunset, the waves, a variety of interesting birds, and people having fun at sea with their pet dogs.

But living by the beach isn't required. You can walk anywhere, and still have some positive effects, as has been demonstrated in "Give Your Ideas Some Legs", a study conducted by Stanford professors Marily Oppezzo and Daniel Schwartz in the *Journal of Experimental Psychology*. They found that those who walked were able to come up with twice as many creative solutions to problems as those who were sitting down, regardless if they walked outdoors or indoors.

However, if you feel that you need more stimulation, find livelier places to walk. It may even be worth driving to your downtown area, or a more interesting part of your town, if it motivates you to actually make this a new habit in your life. Of course, beyond simply the creative benefits, walking is good for your overall health too.

There is no right or wrong way to go about the walking habit, but personally my walks average about 30-40 minutes, and I do it 4-5 days a week, usually. A key is to learn to enjoy the walking for its own sake. I will brainstorm during my walks, but someone else may prefer to simply enjoy the walk and then brainstorm after, which seems perfectly reasonable as well. The research supports that either way can be beneficial for your creativity.

I'm not sure why this works. But there are many possible reasons. When you walk, you are in a constant change of body motion – you are never still. In fact, not a single part of your body is really still. Also, the environment is constantly shifting. You aren't just viewing a static background. It is constantly moving and changing as you walk. As trivial as this may seem, I think walking forces multiple parts of your brain to get active, which stimulates your creative ability.

To add more reasons why, there are many unpredictable elements, such as the chance that you come across a new area, or that you meet someone new or even someone you already know and have an interesting conversation. You may see interesting animals, insects, plants, or other life which can be inspiring. Also, you are moving, but not so fast that you can't process what happens in the background. There is scenery, but it probably isn't so compelling that it distracts you from any new and interesting thoughts you might have.

I read a book called *Daily Rituals* by Mason Currey, which is how I first realized just how major this pattern of walking was in highly productive and creative people's lives. According to the book, some notable people who walked in their daily routines were Ludwig van Beethoven, Frédérick Chopin, Sigmund Freud, Carl Jung, William Faulkner, B. F. Skinner, Immanuel Kant, Franz Kafka, Woody Allen, George Gershwin, René Descartes, Franz Schubert, Victor Hugo, Charles Dickens, Charles Darwin, Nathaniel Hawthorne, Leo Tolstoy, Georgia O'Keeffe, Sergey Rachmaninoff, Albert Einstein, Jackson Pollock, and Oliver Sacks.

These were just some of the people with walking habits mentioned in the book. In total, there were 50 people who had a regular walking habit out of the 161 people profiled. This was the most frequent routine among all of the names included. Keep in mind that the focus of the book was not walking itself. The goal was simply to look at the daily habits of some of the most creative and accomplished people. In my reading, it was clear that walking was the single most reoccurring habit that these people performed in their lives.

The research hasn't yet caught up to exactly *why* walking works. It appears to work on helping creativity whether it's indoors or outdoors. I prefer outdoors when I can, but if it's too cold, hot, or rainy (the weather can't always be perfect for walking) you may want to try getting a treadmill or going to the gym to keep up with the habit. I hope you are convinced that it does work – according to my own experience, the scientific research, and the anecdotes put forth in "Morning Rituals". Sometimes, it's good enough to know that something *does work* – when there is this much support, and we can wait for the scientists to catch up and show exactly *why it works* in the years to come.

Tip #8: Realize That One of the Most Fruitful Parts of Life is NOT Knowing How Things Will Turn Out

From everything we are taught from a young age, it seems as if our goal is to gain control of life. As if life were a horse and we needed to ride it successfully to wherever we wish to go. Consider riding a horse as a metaphor for our lives. We are instructed to see the landscape, see exactly where we want to guide the horse, then to ride it there, and accomplish the things we want.

But the creative style is somewhat different. The creative style says it's okay not to know. It's okay to not have a complete vision of what you wish to accomplish, of how you will get there, of what other people will think of it, or of exactly what the results will be in the end…. It's all okay. And we should be fine with this, because some of these creative ventures will be flops, but some will be so immensely successful that it will be unbelievable. Not knowing the outcomes ahead of time will lead us to have such ups and downs.

Allow me to continue with the "horse of life" metaphor that we are all riding on. Let's say you are creative and you are riding this horse. There are plenty successful paths you see. They are all clearly laid out with signs that say – "this way to success" or "this path works, it's tried and true". Then there are other paths you see, which don't yet exist. It would be up to you to start this new path and see if it leads to anything good. The creative people will go ahead and take this risk…

…and it can be exhilarating. They don't know what will happen, but they are willing to accept this. Failure isn't the worst thing that can happen to a person. Failures are temporary. Then you get to come back with the knowledge of what doesn't work, so you can correct your path and find a better direction. Or better yet, you may discover some great treasure that had escaped everyone else since they stayed on safer paths.

What are Ide...

As a refresher, the fo...
at the beginning of the b...

Idea hacks are systems that ...
with much less effort. I've had m...
trying to come up with new ideas,
shortcuts, to overcome those problem...
up with new ideas regardless of whether
demotivated. Even if you feel bored, unins...
at home on a rainy day, idea hacks provide you...
help you to come up with ideas right away.

These hacks simply allow you to release the creativit...
you. Most of us have a natural creative ability that is not...
For many years, we may have assumed that we were simp...
tive, believing we did not have the eye or knowledge or instin...
ate, but this is untrue. The idea hacks mentioned in this sectio...
meant to help you come up with new ideas regardless of backgrou...
circumstance, or even the type of project you are working on.

I have personally used and tested all of these systems, and they have
collectively helped me to generate thousands of ideas. I don't claim all
of my ideas are the best, but better ones will come with more practice
in generating them. There is no magic machine that will give you brilliant ideas. The best we can do is get better at coming up with more of
them and then identify which are the best ones that we want to apply.
Also, of course, a way to help come up with more ideas is to gain
knowledge and information in your field or area that you wish to be
creative in. At the very least, building an understanding of your area
will help you evaluate whether you have come up with good ideas in
the first place.

Before we learn more about these idea hacks, I want to note one final
thing. The example ideas in these sections are not always truly creative.
This means they are not necessarily high in originality and quality. But

Idea Hacks

...a Hacks?

...lowing paragraph is exactly the same as you read
...ook.

...help you to come up with creative ideas
...share of difficulties and blocks when
...and so I came up with hacks, or
...With idea hacks, you can come
...you feel mentally blocked or
...ired, or if you are trapped
...with a shortcut that will

...already within
...being utilized.
...not crea-
...to cre-
...are
...d,

...ow which are highly creative, and focus your attention on implementing those. Now, let's begin learning about specific idea hacks you can get started using right away.

Alphabet (Soup)

Description of the Idea Hack

This idea hack is one of my favorites. Why? It is very simple to use. You don't need to learn a complicated mnemonic device or system that will take up your valuable time. You already know the alphabet, so getting started will be easy.

With the alphabet idea hack, all you do is run through the alphabet letter by letter to come up with ideas that start with each letter of the alphabet. As a side tip, if you get tired of running through the alphabet in order every time, you can go through it in reverse order too. If you are in the mood for dinner, you might even cook yourself up some alphabet soup and go through the letters in your soup one at a time to come up with new ideas. As an alternative you can also run through the letters in the order of your own name, or the order of the names of friends and family.

This prime, or stimulus for coming up with ideas is so common that most children know it by the age of four or five. Why is this a good way to prime your ideas and get them flowing? There are 26 letters in the alphabet, which can help you come up with about 20 ideas per cycle. No one will expect you to have great success with letters like X and Z, so don't worry about those too much. This is a creativity tool, but also a sort of memory system. You will want to have a wide range of knowledge to pull ideas from, but going through the letters one by one will help you catch those ideas that you might not have thought of so easily. The more knowledge you have, the more ideas you will be able to pull from your memory. Many people don't realize this, but memory and creativity are actually closely connected.

With the alphabet system, you may have the vaguest question or idea as a starting point, and still use it successfully. All creativity needs some basic starting point. For example, what are you trying to come up with ideas in? Perhaps you want to be more creative in your workplace, invent something, or create a piece of art, but you don't have a clear picture on what exactly you want to accomplish. Even if this is the case, you can make progress with the alphabet idea hack.

I like to use this idea hack in sessions. I will identify the topic I want more ideas in, then I will sit down and come up with *at least* one idea for every letter. I cut myself a break on some of the more difficult ones, but in the end I'll usually have 30 or so ideas anyway in a brief session that lasts a few minutes. If the ideas aren't good enough, I'll run a new session the next day, and repeat over and over as needed.

Best Situations to Use

This is a good all-around idea hack, useful in most situations where you need new ideas. However, it relies somewhat on your memory, to recall related words, concepts, and ideas that make sense for your goal. This will be a better system to use as you gain more knowledge in your field, and perhaps you get to the point where you have most of the information you need somewhere in your brain, but getting the ideas to flow out takes some effort.

Also, if you need to come up with a massive number of ideas fast, the alphabet primes will help you create an exhaustive list of all your ideas, since every word that exists starts with one of the 26 letters in the alphabet.

I have listed this idea hack first on purpose. Although very simple, it is highly effective and I routinely use it to help generate new ideas. I often start with this idea hack, and if I need more ideas, I will then move on to others.

Example

To use a classic problem (or cliché) scenario, let's suppose you are stranded on a deserted island. You have crash landed and your plane is destroyed. You are the only person there and you need to survive and make plans to get out of there and back home. To get some ideas, let's use the alphabet idea hack. Here are some ideas I came up with.

- A – amplify my voice – is there something I can do to accomplish this and possibly get attention from any boats that might pass nearby?
- B – bananas – is there some natural growing food I can eat?
- C – container – is there something I can use to capture rainwater to drink?
- D – diligent – I'll have to be very persistent, and not give up, no matter what
- E – entertainment – you will have to find ways to entertain yourself, to keep morale up
- F – food – what are some good sources of food here?
- G – grubs – you might have to consider expanding your definition of food, and eat insects if necessary
- H – highlands – is there high land I can get to, where I might be more visible to rescuers?
- I – ink – is there ink or any way for me to write something down, to get attention or for people to at least know I was here?
- J – Jimmy – can I find a metal tool to help jimmy (force) open any wreckage from the plane? (assuming there is wreckage) – to have access to food and supplies

Exercises to Try

For the following exercises, consider ideas that start with different letters of the alphabet (A-Z) as you come up with ideas.

- Finish the example above, and come up with ideas K-Z (or at least some letters) for what to do on a deserted island
  - Hint: remember that they don't have to be the best ideas ever. Come up with something that could be useful and move on to the next letter. Also, K is a more challenging letter. Feel free to start at L.

- What are some alternative uses for a brick?

- What are some ideas for new baby names (which you have never heard before)?

- What are some ideas for how to write something down without a pen/pencil/marker?

- What are some ideas for how to break out of a car if you are trapped inside, and the doors are jammed and locked?

Questions Galore

Description of the Idea Hack

With this system, you will simply ask as many questions as you can come up with. We will work on bringing out your curiosity, as curiosity and creativity are closely linked. When you come up with questions, it doesn't feel like you are being very creative, but you will actually be directing your mind to look at new possible ideas. In a sense, you will be creating your own prompts to look into further.

Many of us don't realize the full power of questions. But imagine you are in a room of a thousand people. You step up to the front of everyone with a microphone in hand, and you ask a simple question. The question could be anything at all. Suppose if you ask "Where will you be tomorrow at this exact time?" Suddenly, you are in control of the minds of everyone in the room. They are coming up with ideas, all of them, for what they will be doing the following day.

The point here is that whatever questions you come up with will direct your mind intensely to solving those problems and questions. It makes sense think up a variety of questions, and then to think up possible creative ideas or solutions to them.

Best Situations to Use

When dealing with any kind of problem where you feel that your focus needs to be redirected toward something more important, as if you are missing something and you aren't sure what. Asking good questions can help redirect your focus toward where it really matters. Generally, if you feel unsatisfied with your current direction of ideas, or current understanding of a problem, it will be a good time to enter a questioning mode. Questions will help you highlight important parts of the problem that you may have overlooked, and that are worth considering as you come up with new ideas.

Perhaps you have gotten ahead of yourself and taken a creative project on a path that led to a dead end. You aren't sure where you went wrong. This would be a good time to start asking questions about what you could have done or should have done differently. Such questions will lead to new ideas and help get yourself back on track.

Example

In this scenario, let's imagine you are working on coming up with ideas for a completely new transportation system, to perhaps provide better solutions for overpopulated areas. We can only build bigger roads for so long. After a while, we simply have too many people in too many cars, and perhaps it's time for a change in how we transport ourselves.

You ask questions like:

Do we *all* need to drive cars?

This question leads you to think of how cars take up a large amount of space, and often only one person is driving a vehicle, wasting a lot of that space. You consider if we should make it illegal to drive alone, or only allow certain privileged drivers to have that right, to practically make it a requirement to carpool or use public transportation.

How attractive is our public transportation system?

This question leads you to think of how public transportation usually involves long times waiting for a bus, the buses take too long to get to their destination, and the routes are fairly limited, not going on the paths many people need to get to and from work. You consider if more investments could be put in public transportation, to help decongest the roads. One idea is to make the interiors more comfortable and also to artistically design the exteriors of the buses to make them the cool thing to ride.

Would it help if more people walked or rode bicycles, or stopped driving altogether?

You realize it's pretty unlikely to get people to stop driving, but this question leads you to thinking that you could offer benefits for people who walk or ride bicycles. You could add bicycle lanes to most places, nice sidewalks, and give tax credits to those who stop owning a vehicle. You could start a community-wide challenge or contest to have people put monitors on their ankles or bicycles and receive prizes for having some of the most miles walked/run or miles driven in their bicycles.

Exercises to Try

For the following exercises, consider asking many questions as you come up with ideas.

- If a large meteor is at risk of impacting the Earth, what can we can do to stop it?
    - o Hint: Ask questions about how we could direct it away from the Earth, destroy it, or break it into smaller pieces

- How would you create a new social marketing platform that can compete with Facebook and Twitter?

- What would you do to create a new video game capable of competing with some of the most popular ones available?

- How would you help your child have the most successful lemonade stand in the state?

- Where would you start if you wanted to design your front or backyard in a way no one else was (consider plants, trees, sidewalk layout, ornaments, etc.)?

Worst Idea

Description of the Idea Hack

When experiencing a creative block and you can no longer come up with much of anything, often the reason we have trouble coming up with new ideas is because we stop them as they are forming. I believe it is a natural process for us to come up with new ideas. A block shows that something has changed to obstruct this natural process. One of the changes may be that you are evaluating yourself too harshly. Doing this creates two big problems for your creativity. If you evaluate your ideas harshly as they are coming out of you, they essentially get destroyed before the idea has a chance to even be fully conceived. The other problem is that if you are evaluating yourself and your ideas harshly, this means you are essentially punishing yourself for coming up with ideas. Anyone at all who is punished for something, will clearly not want to do it again.

Here is a solution to these problems that will help you to get unblocked, and also to come up with new and fresh ideas. You may not understand it or agree with it at first, but keep an open mind here.

Purposely come up with the worst ideas that you possibly can.

Make this your goal. You will be surprised to find that sometimes there are hidden gems in these supposedly awful ideas. The other thing is you will quickly lose your mental block. A common scenario is that you start coming up with awful ideas. They may make you laugh at how wild they are at first, but after you come up with so many, you'll find yourself thinking things like "hey that's so crazy... but it just might work". Even if all of your ideas from this are complete duds, complete failures, you will prove to yourself that you are not blocked. You will see that being blocked was only an unnatural temporary state you fell into. Then when you get your bad ideas out of the way, you can start coming up with some good ones.

The other thing you will learn in this process is that there is nothing to fear from bad ideas. They aren't going to come to life and haunt you. No one is going to give you a failing grade for them. All you've lost is a few minutes of your time, but it's a good exercise anyway. Coming up with ideas, any ideas at all, is a great exercise for your creativity. Any time spent coming up with ideas, even bad ones, is not wasted.

Best Situations to Use

This is a highly useful idea hack for getting creatively unstuck and un-blocked. If there is immense pressure on you to create something, and you feel frozen and unable to make progress, this tool will help you get back on track. It is also useful simply as a creative exercise on its own, to help practice coming up with ideas.

Personally, I have found it to be an entertaining way to think, too. If you periodically think throughout your day, "What is the worst thing I could do here?" or "What is the worst response I could come up with?" then you will not only come up with more creative ideas, but also more interesting ones that can make you and those around you laugh.

Example

Perhaps you want to come up with ideas for a new type of jewelry. You are feeling mentally blocked, unable to come up with something fresh and new, so you decide to come up with the worst ideas you possibly can. Your goal becomes to find ideas for jewelry that no one would probably want to wear.

The ideas start to flow. What if you made jewelry out of coal, the type of black and chalky coal used to cook outdoors. Or what if you made jewelry that was made with mercury, a toxic substance. Perhaps instead of a bracelet to wear around the wrist, you could design body jewelry that was meant to be wrapped around the leg, arm, shoulder, etc., in unusual ways. Or what if the jewelry changed colors depending on the temperature. Another option would be to add an alarm so only one person could wear it, its owner, or it would make an annoying beeping sound nonstop and eventually spray ink if the person didn't take it off.

I will be the first to admit that these are not such great ideas. Although the concept of body jewelry could be interesting – I don't wear jewelry, so I'm not sure if that is a real thing. Anyway, the point of this idea hack was that some of these bad ideas might become inspiring on their own. Trying to figure out a way to make these ideas actually work can lead to surprising results, and prove to you that anything can work, if you are dedicated to making it happen and persistent.

For example, instead of using actual coal, it might be interesting if some jewelry had a coal type of color. Or with mercury, to make it safe, it could be encased protectively, as with the old style thermometers, but perhaps mixed with gold or other kinds of jewelry. Interestingly, even when we make it a goal to come up with bad ideas, some of them can potentially be implemented in creative ways. Lots of good can come from bad ideas. Just give it a try.

If nothing else, they will be good for a laugh, to ease your tensions and reduce your stress, and help prepare you to start coming up with better ideas.

Exercises to Try

For the following exercises, consider the worst ideas you can think of.

- What is the worst idea for how a college student can earn Straight A's?
  - o Hint: Is there a way to accomplish this without even attending class?
- What is the worst idea for a new kind of toaster?
- What is the worst idea for the design of a child's toy gun?
- What is the worst idea for home decorations?
- What is the worst idea for how to build a snowman?

Context

Description of the Idea Hack

With your creative problem, you should consider the full context surrounding it. Often, we get stuck on a problem or can't come up with ideas because we are thinking of our problem too directly or too literally. We tend to neglect clues or cues that come from the environment itself and that may help us to solve the problem in unexpected ways.

We have to consider that there are many different types of contexts. For example, some research such as the article "Physical Order Produces Healthy Choices, Generosity, and Conventionality, Whereas Disorder Produces Creativity" in *Psychological Science* by Kathleen Vohs and her colleagues, has demonstrated that orderly environments guide us toward doing things in line with convention, whereas disorderly environments promote creative thinking and breaking with tradition.

One of the reasons for this is because there will be a rich amount of contextual signals in the "messy" or disordered environment. All of this context can serve as clues for how to solve a problem. Even if the context seems irrelevant, often when working on a tough creative problem, we can find a way to relate things that seem unrelated. Signals coming from the context, from the environment itself, will lead to thinking in new directions that wouldn't have otherwise occurred to us.

I've personally found this idea hack to be quite useful. I'm a cerebral type of person, so I sometimes tend to abandon the real world and get stuck in my own head. This can be helpful for concentration, but it can also be silly when there is a need to be creative, because more often than not we can pick up some convenient creative cues directly from the surroundings. After noticing time and time again the power of environmental cues to help with creative thinking, I decided that I needed to ignore my own mind at times, and pay attention to the surrounding context.

Best Situations to Use

This is a helpful idea hack when you are in an area rich with detail and complexity, or that you find inspiring in some way. It can also be useful when you are in a new area with many objects, designs, or things that you have not seen or experienced before.

Also, contextual cues can be useful in situations that are constantly changing and adaptive, where the context itself does not stay the same. A prime example of this type of context is in social situations. You will come up with more ideas, perhaps ideas for something to say, by examining the context, the situation, and the surrounding atmosphere closely. The context will be all around you, making this idea hack quite simple for anyone to use.

It can also be used in environments where you are so used to everything that nothing seems new anymore. Often times when we feel this way, we are actually ignoring the context because it feels old and boring. But if we look closely, we may find new things to spark our ideas.

Example

Imagine a situation where a friend introduces you to a friend of his, but then your friend has to leave, and you are now alone with this new person you were introduced to. After brief small talk, you aren't sure what else to say, but it would be rude to just walk away.

Thinking of the context of your meeting, you realize both of you know the friend who introduced you, but you don't know how this person knows the friend. As an easy idea, you can ask how she knows him.

Perhaps you also notice some earrings she is wearing, which have an interesting design. You can simply ask her what type of earrings they are, or what they signify, again to have more ideas for conversation.

The gathering you are at is being held for different divisions of your work to meet each other. This is another part of the context of your meeting. You can ask her about which division she works for, or if she is just accompanying your friend.

Other context ideas are mentioning the music that is playing, if someone does something goofy or noteworthy in the area, commenting on decorations, and so forth.

Exercises to Try

For the following exercises, consider the context or situations surrounding the problem as you come up with ideas.

- When you are bored, use the context of what is available in the environment to help you come up with ideas for something to do. Even if you are at home, start exploring and look for something new you had forgotten about.
    - o Hint: Sift through old notebooks or folders, look through cabinets or drawers you haven't checked in a long time, and enter rooms or closets that you rarely use, to start.

- If you want to come up with a product idea, but you don't know where to start, look at your own personal context. What is something you have used where you were dissatisfied with the product or service? What are some ways to improve upon those ideas?

- If you want to work on a new piece of artwork, but you have no idea where to go from here, look at the context of the prior work you have created, of any artists who have influenced you, of what other artists are doing that you know personally, etc.

- If your boss asks you to come up with some new ideas for the next company meeting, walk around the office, looking at people's family photos or paintings on the wall, or bios on the wall of former company leaders, or anything in the surroundings that could help spark new ideas.

- If you are an employer and your employees look worn out but you want them to be more productive, look at the context of what they want or need.

Culture

Description of the Idea Hack

Ask yourself how different cultures would react to the problem or general area you are looking for ideas in. For example, you might consider groups such as Native Americans, Indians, Latinos, Africans, or Asians as broad examples. Of course, if you know the intricacies of specific cultures, you can go deeper into the cultures of specific regions or countries.

For this idea hack, clearly it will be important to have some familiarity with other cultures. If you don't, that is no problem. You might start with reading about cultures, how they live, their history, the priorities they tend to have, rituals or ceremonies that are important to them, their music and art, and any other details you can learn about them. Of course, if you can experience different cultures first-hand and travel, this would be a great bonus to your learning as well. If you just want to gain a broad idea of a culture, sites like Wikipedia may help with this.

Note that most of the idea hacks in this book don't require much extra knowledge. However, if you aren't already well informed on various cultures, you will need to at least do some basic learning about them in order to effectively use this idea hack.

Best Situations to Use

This is a helpful idea hack when you need a completely new way of looking at a problem, or a completely different type of solution to the same problem. Perspectives of different cultures can be wildly different. Some cultures value having more items, some value having less. Some value family, some value work more. Some believe certain professions to be the most prestigious, others will view that same profession as one to be avoided. If you feel that you are too narrow in the way you are looking at a particular problem, and that your background and worldview is keeping you from seeing the full picture, this will be a useful idea hack to use.

Example

Suppose that you are a shoe designer. You want to come up with ideas for a brand new shoe, and you want to revolutionize the shoe industry with something that has wide appeal. Growing up in the United States, you have a pretty well-defined view of what a shoe is, what to expect from them, the price range, and so forth. But to come up with new ideas, you investigate how shoes work in other parts of the world. Looking into other countries, you are saddened to learn that in many areas, people cannot afford shoes. Some of the top brands worn routinely in the US are completely out of the question in other parts of the world, or reserved only for the wealthy.

Looking into what a shoe means for different cultures and places, you realize that the concept of a shoe is somewhat irrelevant in many parts of the world, where shoes are often too expensive and inaccessible to the public. Because of this realization, soon your creative juices start flowing. You ask questions like: What cheaper yet durable materials could I use to make a shoe? How can I get funding for a good cause to get cheap and durable shoes to the people who really need them? Is there a way I can hire people from these struggling countries to design shoes, so the workers earn a good living as well? All of a sudden your mind is moving in directions you would have never considered if you hadn't looked into what shoes mean for other cultures.

Exercises to Try

For the following exercises, consider what might appeal to cultures from around the world as you come up with ideas.

- When decorating, ask "What would other cultures think of this style of decoration?"
    - Hint: How would the Japanese decorate, or Egyptians, or the French?
- What are some ideas for a new sport?
- What are some ideas for things to do on your free time?
- Write a poem on your life.
- Plan a party.

Time Period (Past, Present, and Future)

Description of the Idea Hack

I'm going to state something obvious, but just think of it for a moment. We are all born within only a single time period, and this is all that we get to experience directly. Time is always flowing forward, meaning we can never exit and experience other points of time.

However, thinking about the past can help give us new creative ways of looking at the same things. This may seem like a silly idea at first. The point of creativity is to come up with new, fresh ideas, not to go backward, but forward. This is true, but what if there is an old system that was forgotten, but is now highly relevant? Just because something is old doesn't mean it was bad. Possibly you will come across an idea that was well ahead of its time, and for that reason it died early. You could actually re-discover a great idea through studying the past.

If you still find it dreadful to look to the past for new ideas, perhaps you would be more interested in looking toward the future instead. Of course, the future doesn't exist yet, but that doesn't mean you can't brainstorm what it will be like, in order to discover new ideas. Be prepared to speculate, imagine, and think critically for this to be worthwhile.

The key point with this idea hack is that when you look into the past or the future, you are switching your mode of thought into a completely different frame of operating. Rather than focusing on the current problems and state of things, you will have to shift your focus to looking at the problem from the perspective of another time, what they knew then (or will know), the materials they had (or will have), and so forth. By switching your point of view, you will be more likely to come up with new and interesting ideas.

Best Situations to Use

When you have been applying a specific solution to a problem for a long time, but because of new developments it is simply no longer feasible, this will be a good time to look into what kind of solutions people in the past were using. You may find that the old ways of doing things sparks new ideas in you to make advancements.

Also, if you ever find yourself quite confident, perhaps overconfident, in a solution to a type of problem, it could be useful for you to look into historic solutions to similar kinds of problems. You never know when things will suddenly change and your current solution no longer works. Or, by looking into what people through history did to solve the problem, you may learn of an improvement you can apply to your system, to improve results even further.

Example

Creativity can be used as an anti-boredom tool, so let's use it to solve the problem of boredom itself. What if you are bored, and you need some creative energy, but you are too bored to even know where to start? Maybe you begin to wonder what people used to do when they were bored, or to entertain themselves, before all of this modern technology. For example, before computers, TV, radio, and so forth. What could they have possibly done?

You do some research and you realize there are a countless number of card games in existence, some that no one ever seems to play anymore. People would sit around the piano and listen to someone play, even singing along. Dice games were in vogue for a long time, dating back to ancient cultures. Simply watching nature or birds was something people did. They read books, not needing to consider television or computers as other options of entertainment. Taking all this into account, you come up with a grand way to relieve yourself of boredom. You decide, why not have a pre-1950s themed party where only activities from those eras are allowed? It seems like a creative solution to the problem. You can invite your friends to bring or recommend any activity that fits the theme and time frame.

Exercises to Try

For the following exercises, consider what kind of solutions might make more sense for different time periods as you come up with ideas.

- When you need ideas, consider what someone in the past would have done.
    - o   Hint: if coming up with ideas for a whole new genre of music to create, it makes sense to look at the history of different genres that have existed in music: classical, jazz, rock 'n roll, classic rock, country, etc.

- If you need ideas, consider what changes might happen in the future. For example, could there be better materials, processes, or theories?

- Consider what your own ancestors might have done if they had the same problem as you.

- Ask what you yourself might have done if facing the same problem when you were younger, in the past, or what you might do in the future about it.

- When you can't think of a good idea, try to trick your brain, and ask "If I were in the future and this problem were already solved, what would the solution look like?"

Abandonment

Description of the Idea Hack

Whatever your creative domain or project is, stop a minute and think about some of the key assumptions, conventions, and rules that dictate it. For this idea hack, you will want to know your area well enough that these boundaries are clear. In order to be able to break rules, you will first have to know what they are.

When you have some of those rules in mind, toss them out of your mental window. Make the choice to purposely stop assuming those rigid rules are in place. If the rules and conventions state that things must always work in one particular way, abandon that whole idea. Decide to explore and entertain entirely different ideas that might work instead.

Consider that everyone has certain expectations for what a home looks like. It has windows, doors, it is above ground for the most part, and so forth. Similarly, we have expectations for how we get served at restaurants, for how we should interact with pets, and for how to raise children. This creative system involves throwing such conventions out the window, and looking for specific ways to defy them.

The point with this idea hack is that you may be taking too narrow of a view in making attempts to solve problems creatively. If you operate under all of these rigid assumptions that everyone else is working under, you are very likely to come up with the same old ideas everyone else is having – which of course is not creative. When you get yourself stuck in that small space, you lose the room to express your creative ideas. In order to do so, you will have to be ready to abandon the rules and cast them aside.

Best Situations to Use

This will be a good idea hack to try when you are an expert in an area and you know the rules quite well. You have worked with the conventions and rules for so long in your domain that they have become all too obvious to you. They are a natural part of you, like breathing, so it *seems* there is absolutely no reason to question them. Perhaps you have become too comfortable with understanding the current system and having it work for you. But if you want to come up with new and creative ideas to advance further, this is the time when you need to be prepared to set aside all of those things you know. Then, you can explore whether there are other ways to make progress that you have overlooked.

Example

Let's say we are working on ideas for how to build a new type of car model. This example should be fun and interesting because there are many things we tend to expect about cars. All we have to do is pick apart any of these things we typically expect, and abandon the idea to search for new ones. Notice that focusing on parts of the car first will keep things simple, so we can focus on specific areas instead of just the general idea of coming up with ideas for a new car model.

We can start with the steering wheel. Pretty much all cars have them, but let's abandon the idea that we *must* have a steering wheel. An idea is that perhaps we could use a joystick instead, as is used in video games and in some helicopters. How about the tires? Do they need to be shaped like normal wheels? Could we use spherical ball-shaped tires, or some other kind of new design? Also, perhaps instead of regular air bags, they could also have foam or gel inside of them to help lessen an impact, instead of just air.

As you can see, you might end up with some weirder, stranger ideas, because we are looking for things that are outside the expected system – abandoning the old ways. But that is okay, anything that gets your creativity flowing is good.

Exercises to Try

For the following exercises, abandon conventions and your prior expectations as you come up with ideas.

- What are some alternative ideas for a home design?
  - Hint: How could you abandon the need for windows? Can you abandon the need for the typical upside-down V-shaped roof?
- What are some alternative ideas for how to make a burger?
- What are some alternative uses for a paperclip?
- What is an alternative type of hat that could be made?
- What is an alternative design for a chair?

Necessity

Description of the Idea Hack

When you are searching for a new idea, or you are facing a creative problem, ask yourself "What is absolutely essential that I must have to solve this?" Think of something where without it, you would be unable to make progress. But the key is to avoid over-defining the problem. Sometimes we assume we need something, but we really don't. Be sure to only consider the things that are truly needed.

This idea hack is meant to help you focus on the critical parts of a problem. When in a creative frame of mind, searching too broadly can actually be a bad thing. You may end up with all kinds of wild ideas that are completely irrelevant and unhelpful. Instead of allowing the mind to wander aimlessly, you can be more productive by focusing on the key things that need to be met for your idea to work. This way, you can discard the irrelevant parts that are not worth exploring.

This system is basically the opposite of the Abandonment idea hack. Instead of looking at completely abandoning a framework, we are looking for what parts are truly essential that we need to keep. With Abandonment, we're not necessarily concerned with keeping anything. If you are creating a new burger (using Abandonment), you can end up with a burger that uses flatbread instead of buns, and tofu instead of burger. But if we look at this through the perspective of what is necessary, we might define the burger as needing red meat, burger buns, and lettuce and tomato. Anything else is fair game to change. The bonus is that you will end up with appropriate, practical solutions that make sense for the problem at hand.

Best Situations to Use

This idea hack is especially useful when you are dealing with a serious problem that has clear time frames. In other words, there is some pressure for you to realistically solve the problem fast and arrive at a good solution. In looking at the parts that are absolutely necessary, you will avoid moving along paths that will waste time and resources.

Example

In this example scenario, you are on a committee to look at how agriculture might be possible on other planets. This involves a human space program with the goal of colonizing Mars and possibly more planets in the future. First, since this is such a serious problem, and you are on an important committee, you decide to look at the parts of the problem that are absolutely essential. From there, you hope to come up with some good ideas that can be used to start farming land and growing crops on other planets.

So you ask: What is absolutely necessary in order to farm on other planets? These are things that would make your task impossible if you did not have them. Of course, there must be sunlight or suitable artificial lighting. There must be water. There should probably be soil, but actually you think, it's not necessarily required because there are hydroponic plants grown on Earth, often indoors. Hydroponics is a process of growing plants in sand, gravel or liquid and with added nutrients but without soil.

The task so far seems easy, and you think you are probably done with figuring out the necessary things that must be there. But then you realize something you almost forgot, because it doesn't come into play on Earth. You realize that you probably need a certain level of gravity to grow a plant. You don't know what gravity level you might need, but it will likely need to be close to the Earth's. You call some astronomers and decide to collaborate to test what gravity is essential for most plants. That way you will know all of the necessities which must be met to solve the creative problem of growing plants on other planets.

You feel good because you are on the right track. When all of these essentials are figured out, then you'll be fully prepared to come up with good creative ideas to plant crops on other planets. Some other ideas that are also worth considering, which could be essential to solving the problem, are temperature, radiation levels, the need for certain bacteria or any other organisms that promote the life of plants, and that the plants are able to obtain required nutrients.

With this idea hack, rather than waste time and energy coming up with irrelevant ideas, you can first figure out what is necessary to solving your problem. Then you can use your creative energy to figuring out how to get all of those essentials fulfilled. In this case, it may require building new inventions or founding new systems for accomplishing the goal of planting on other planets.

Exercises to Try

For the following exercises, consider what would be absolutely essential to solving the problem as you come up with ideas.

- What are some ideas for a new recipe? Ask yourself what would be absolutely necessary to be defined as that type of dish?
    - Hint: for spaghetti, most people would define it as needing some kind of meat that is cut up or ground, noodles, and tomato sauce.
- What are some ideas for a new game?
- What are some ideas for a new design for a swimsuit?
- What are some ideas for a new kind of alien species (as in for a science fiction movie)?
- What are some ideas for a new style of music?

Nature

Description of the Idea Hack

The reason nature can be so inspiring is that it deals with many of the same issues that humans also deal with. Consider the mosquito. No matter how annoying the creature is, perhaps it was a source of inspiration for the original creators of successful syringes. Think of it. The mosquito itself acts as a natural syringe, as its needle mouth is designed to remove blood from its victims. The syringe does the same thing, but for medical purposes instead of to feed on us.

As another example, consider dams. They were created before humans ever made them, by beavers. Perhaps some of the first human dam builders got the idea from these natural dam builders. Advancements have occurred in flight and aviation technology by studying how birds do it so well. In some cases, the natural productions of nature are actually used by us for our own purposes. Of course there is food that grows naturally, and paper we get from trees, and medical compounds we get from plants. And then there is the silk worm, whose produced silk is used in fabrics and clothing.

Specifically, this idea hack will involve looking at nature's way of solving a problem, to see what kind of ideas we can get from it. You can actually go out and observe nature, or it could be helpful to search YouTube videos of any specific animals, insects, or plants that could be of interest. Or you can always use Google, and search [creative problem] + words like "nature's solution" or "animal kingdom".

By seeing how nature tends to solve problems you have had, you will come away with new and interesting ideas. Of course, sometimes we aren't aware that there exists a solution for a problem until we see it in nature. Throughout history, humans have often come across nature's solutions to a problem just by chance. However, you do not need to rely solely on chance. To increase your ability to use this idea hack, it would be useful to watch nature programs or to go out and watch nature on your own. It helps if you already have a creative problem in mind as you do so.

Best Situations to Use

If you are interested in physical creations that involve engineering, building, or construction of some kind, you could find it highly useful to study how nature has dealt with such problems. You may study animals that build things, or animals with natural features which allow them to accomplish things we normally cannot.

For example, plants in nature often provide healing properties or make us feel better in some way. Anyone interested in new chemicals or medicines could benefit from studying nature.

Also, some species of jellyfish such as *Turritopsis dohrnii* have been found to have the ability to be biologically immortal, growing old then becoming young again, in cycles. They are capable of dying from predators, but they do not die of old age itself. Someone interested in longevity or immortality could possibly get some interesting ideas from studying animals which are able to live for so long.

Example

Consider a situation where you are concerned with the lack of clean water to drink around the world, and you want to work on this problem. You think first, the problem isn't necessarily cleaning the water. After all, in nature, you never see animals cleaning water and using filtering systems like humans do. Instead, animals tend to go toward water sources that are cleaner when possible. So you reframe the question to, "How do we collect clean water?"

You start thinking of ways that nature collects clean water, and you realize there are cacti (or cactuses) in deserts all around the world right now, collecting water inside of them. Of course, you don't want to go out and break all of these cacti open to get fresh water. Doing that would be impractical, because no one wants to go to a desert just to get their water. They would die of thirst on the way. Instead, you start wondering if you could create something like the cactus, but not so prickly. It would act as a reliable container and be safe from outside contaminants, but still collect rainwater inside of it.

You think, the cactus somehow manages to do this naturally, so there must be an invention similar to it which could be created, with the aim of gathering clean water for people to drink. This will require some investigation. Of course, purification is another problem that still needs to be sorted out, but we seem to be on the right track, collecting relatively clean rainwater and keeping it protected. The point here is that by investigating how nature solves problems more deeply, we will be able to get creative ideas which we can take action on to solve similar problems for ourselves.

Exercises to Try

For the following exercises, consider how something in nature would approach these problems.

- How would you make a safety device to scare predators (human, animal, or otherwise)?
    - Hint: Consider what nature's solution is to scaring predators away. What does the elephant do to scare animals away? What does the lion do?
- How would you create a parachute?
- How would you create a machine that digs for you?
- How would you design scuba slippers for diving?
- How would you climb the side of a building without using a ladder?

Perspective

Description of the Idea Hack

Often, when working on creative problems, we find ourselves locked into one perspective. You may find it helpful to consider how people would look at the problem from other perspectives. If you are working on creating a new product, try viewing how a client would see it. What would they think? Contact a professional who normally takes an alternative approach to your own, and ask what they think. If they are unavailable, imagine what they would tell you. Or consider the situation from the perspective of an investor. Whether or not you are seeking investors, it could be interesting to imagine what they would say about your product. Would they think it is worth investing in? Would it be worth their time?

Taking other perspectives helps us get out of the one track mind that we sometimes develop. Being inclined to take a single perspective doesn't mean we are selfish. It is actually natural since we always view the world through our own eyes, and therefore we will tend to analyze and think of everything through this single outlook. It will take some practice to start considering alternative viewpoints, and then it will take a bit more practice to get good at actually knowing what people from other perspectives will tend to think. But this is highly worthwhile. You will get better not only at generating ideas, but evaluating them as well, with this idea hack.

A key part of taking someone else's perspective is to not do this superficially. Commit to truly getting inside their mind and thought processes. You have to learn to put your own perspectives and preconceptions aside for a moment. With enough practice, you may feel as if you have the power to actually step into the mind of someone else, and know what they are thinking, why they are doing what they do, and what their concerns are. Then, when you understand these things, you can shift back to your own mindset, and begin generating solutions to tackle all of these problems.

Getting deep into another perspective will probably involve asking questions such as: What would be my biggest concern, in their position? What would be my number one objective? How would I feel about this product/service as it is now? Would it be appealing to me if I were rich or poor, well-educated versus not, from the city or the country, etc.?

Best Situations to Use

You will want to use this idea hack when you have gotten too locked into one way of seeing things, and you find it hard to imagine another way of thinking or perceiving. If you are often surrounded by people who tend to think in a similar way, you will need to be careful to consider outside perspectives. When surrounded by people who think similarly, it's easy to assume everyone else thinks the same way, which is actually rarely the case. You don't want to be shocked to find that other people think in a completely different way and that you have ignored their valid viewpoints. When you consider these other perspectives, it will help you to make sure you are not overlooking important ideas.

Example

If you are creating a new car model, and you are mainly interested in having it look cool, don't assume that this will be everyone's main concern. Stop to think about different perspectives, such as what different customers might want. For instance, some might want safety, others prefer looks, and still others may be worried about fuel efficiency. Parents will be concerned with having enough space for the whole family, and others might want more cargo space to move around furniture or other items. Of course, you may not be able to create one car that appeals to every single perspective, but in considering some of them you will open yourself up to having more creative ideas and to perhaps be able to design a car that is more appealing to a wide variety of people, as opposed to just a small number that only care about the appearance.

In this case, a solution is to try to cover many bases, to create a car that appeals to a larger population. You end up deciding to design the car at a medium size, to help conserve fuel but still have enough cargo space for most needs. You make sure it is built as safely as possible, with children's safety in mind as well. You also do what you can to give the model a unique look that is likely to appeal to many buyers. So it still looks attractive, but that was not the sole focus of building it either.

By focusing on appealing to a wide range of perspectives, you will need to find creative solutions to meet a variety of needs. You should challenge yourself to consider two opposite perspectives all at once. For example, keep in mind the experience of a young, large single man, and an older, smaller woman with a family. Can you design the car that appeals to both? You might ask questions such as "What is the common ground between most different perspectives that all people seem to want in a car?" or "Are there designs that can appeal to both the man and woman in this case?"

In case it isn't clear, this idea hack will stimulate and exercise your creative ideas because you will need to find new solutions to appeal to different perspectives. Of course, in some business decisions you may simply choose one type of market and ignore the perspectives of outside groups. For those types of businesses, you may prefer to use this idea hack to consider other perspectives, such as that of investors or even the perspective of other businesses, and what their reaction may be to your new car design.

Exercises to Try

For the following exercises, consider other perspectives, such as of a client, boss, coworker, parent, and so forth, as you come up with ideas.

- What is an idea for an alarm clock made for young children under five? Keep in mind that this population tends to have a difficult time getting up in the morning, but at the same time they often have more sensitive hearing and may be prone to crying if disturbed. (I know such an invention probably wouldn't have much practical use, since parents usually wake up their children if necessary, but this is still a useful creative exercise.)

    o Hint: If you were a child, you might *not* prefer a loud buzzer. You also might want something that rewards you when you stop the alarm and wake up, or you could just fall back asleep otherwise.

- What is an idea for how to stop smoking when someone has smoked chronically for 20+ years?

- What is an idea for a musical type instrument designed for dogs or cats to play?

- What is an idea for a system to solve the problem of human litter and trash that ends up invading the natural habitat of wildlife?

- Spend some time observing people or animals, and imagining life through their perspective. Avoid imposing your own prior beliefs on them.

Reversal (Go in reverse, work backward, or look in the opposite direction)

Description of the Idea Hack

Whatever problem you are trying to solve, make a point to look at it in the opposite direction, or going in reverse. This can help open up your thinking to new possibilities you might never have otherwise considered.

Reversing a problem or looking at it backward is something most of us don't think to do. Often, it will seem silly to do so, and many times it may not seem especially useful. But this system can provide useful insights and is well worth trying, to help come up with new ideas.

This idea hack can be used in a variety of ways, depending on the problem or on what you are trying to achieve. For a novelist, it may involve working backward, and forming your ending before arriving at the beginning. For an inventor who is working on a new clock design, it may involve reverse-engineering, or taking apart several other clocks, to learn how a variety of different designs work. For someone stuck on a new business service they are trying to form, this may involve looking at the problem the opposite way. Instead of asking how you can provide a similar service as your competitors, perhaps you can ask what customers are looking for that is not being met by anyone else. Instead of focusing on your own business perspective, you can shift and focus on the customer.

Whatever the problem or scenario is, flip it, reverse it, and approach it in the opposite way from what would normally be expected.

Best Situations to Use

This idea hack is worthwhile when you are working on one of those problems that you are completely stuck on, unsure of what else you can try. In such a case, you should consider reversing everything. Often, this won't be the first idea hack we are inclined to try. But if you have run through several other idea hacks and you aren't getting the results you would like, this one will be well worth trying out.

Example

Imagine that you work at a company that creates kitchen supplies. As the creative designer, you have been assigned with the task of coming up with an idea for an oven mitten that can withstand extremely hot temperatures and is extra protective, beyond what is traditionally expected. This is in efforts to attract more customers, especially those with more sensitive skin or who fear getting burned while cooking.

Typically, when given a task, even creative ones, we will approach the problem directly. This often works well for traditional problems, such as math problems, where a set approach is known to work. But creative tasks require different approaches that are not always so direct. The direct approach here would be to try to come up with ideas for how to make an oven mitten more heat resistant, since that is the task given.

However, this idea hack involves completely reversing the problem, which can take us in several different directions. Let's go in reverse, and instead of focusing on the oven mitt, focus on what is actually hot that it is attached to. This is a reversal, because when cooking, you will probably get your pan, put it on the stove, then it will get hot, and then you will need your oven mitt. If we go back in time a bit, the pan is put on the stove first, and the pan is what gets hot. Why are we focusing on the mitt? Maybe we should look into pans where the handle would not get so hot to begin with, perhaps built to be more heat resistant.

This thought process essentially flips the problem away from the mitt, to the pan. It creates new possibilities and directions for the company to go in. Perhaps they can create a new mitt *and* a new pan, or perhaps a new heat resistant pan alone will be enough. Since the pan solution would be more convenient, the company decides to start there.

Instead of reversing or going backward, another way to apply this idea hack is to look in the opposite direction from what is expected. For the above example, this would involve asking a question such as "How can I solve this problem (of protecting people from burns) *without* focusing on the oven mitt itself?" This would likely lead us in a similar direction, to wonder how we could build a more heat resistant pan.

Notice that going in reverse or looking in the opposite direction are unique processes, but they tend to lead to similar results. Because of this, they are both mentioned under this idea hack.

Exercises to Try

For the following exercises, consider looking at the problem in terms of its opposite, going in reverse, or working backward as you come up with ideas.

- Consider if you were a slow typist. What are some ideas for how to increase your words per minute typed?

  - Hint: Instead of focusing on increasing your speed, we could focus on the opposite and look at the keyboard instrument, and if you could create a new design for a keyboard that would help you type faster. Or maybe you can dictate the information instead of typing, into a special software that automatically writes it out for you.

- When dealing with a problem, flip the question to its opposite. For example, instead of "How can I find this address and meet my friends with this map?", how about "How would I be able to find this address and meet my friends *without* the map?"

- For a product that you use every day, ask how you could accomplish the same task without using that product. Imagine that it just disappeared.

- For the next creative task you begin, start from the end if possible, and work your way toward the beginning.

- For the next movie that you watch, imagine your own alternate ending, middle, and beginning, in that order.

Change the Order

Description of the Idea Hack

Perhaps you have tried the Reversal idea hack and you did not get the results you would have liked. You found that just looking at the problem in a backward order didn't necessarily help much. In that case, changing up the order in other interesting ways may be helpful.

People are generally very ordered. Many things about our lives have structure. Think to the products and services we tend to use on an everyday basis. The more ordered and reliable they are, the more likely we are to continue using them. Clearly, order is very highly valued, and often with good reason, because it helps us to be more efficient, meeting our goals head on.

However, sometimes when we are coming up with creative ideas, our need for order can get in the way of our progress. We tend to get fixated on a system or process needing to happen in one set order. This inhibits our ability to come up with new and interesting ideas. A common theme in coming up with creative ideas is that we should lose the need to restrict a problem into a tiny space. We should be prepared to expand our viewpoint as to how we look at the problem.

For this idea hack, when there is a process or system you are working with, simply try changing up the order. Be open to thinking of the process in a completely new way, rather than always looking at it as the same old process you have always been used to. Even if you come across an ordering that seems ridiculous, like it could never possibly work, just allow yourself to entertain the idea that maybe it could work. You may be surprised to find that simply by changing steps, such as doing the first step second, or your third step first, you come across a new and great idea that had been completely overlooked.

Best Situations to Use

As already mentioned, this is a good idea hack to use if you have already tried the Reversal idea hack and not gotten the results you would have liked.

Also, this is a useful hack when you are working on a creative problem that involves a series of steps, or a process, and there is a natural ordering to it that everyone is used to. Perhaps this order is so natural, or so ingrained that no one appears to question it. It is exactly at this point when you *should* pick apart the ordering and question it.

Example

Consider if you were a greeting card writer. Every day, your employer sends you a topic that he needs more cards for, such as for a Christmas letter, a birthday for a nine year old, a college graduation, get well soon, etc. You receive the topic, and your job is to write a new and interesting card. As the next step, your employer finds a graphic design to match what you have written. This has mostly worked well, but lately you feel that you are running out of ideas. You have written up so many birthday cards that it is difficult to come up with something new.

You decide another order may help your creative idea process. Instead of writing first, and then having your employer find an image to go with the writing, you think your ability to come up with ideas could work so much better if you changed it around, and had your employer send you an image first, and then you could write something to fit the theme of the image. Your employer is happy to try out this change. Now, you will fit your writing to match whichever image he chooses. After this change, you find that your writing is much more original and appropriate to the design of the final cards.

Exercises to Try

For the following exercises, consider looking at the problem in a different order as you come up with ideas.

- Ask yourself if the order of daily routines (or of your daily tasks) is really the best. Could you flip things around and get better results?

  o Hint: Could you do something at night instead of in the morning, or vice versa?

- Write a short story or a micro-story, and ask yourself if the order of events could be moved around to improve it.

- Draw a picture in one order, such as left to right, figure and then background, or however you choose. Then, draw the same picture again in a different order and compare the results.

- Take something simple apart, such as an old mechanical pencil sharpener (something that won't cause you problems if you accidentally break it). Then put it together again, of course using a different order.

- Try something that you always do in one order, in a different order. It could be something simple like the way you drive to work, the way you plan your day, the things you do on a date, etc.

Abridge / Detail

Description of the Idea Hack

When you have a creative problem you are working on, try to redefine the problem in a completely new way. If there are so many details and fine parts to the problem that you have to consider, and it is getting overwhelming, try making the process more concise and only look at the big picture parts, perhaps condensing a 20 step process down to three phases. This will help to redefine the whole problem and shape your way of thinking in a new direction, which will give you more ideas.

On the other hand, if you are working on a fairly simple system or process, and you don't feel like you have much to be creative about because of the simplicity, start looking at the problem through a magnifying glass, so to speak. Examine every tiny detail, no matter how irrelevant it may seem. Something hidden in the cracks there may give you a new clue as to what your next steps will need to be. If you have seen or read Sherlock Holmes, his approach may provide a hint, of needing to dig through and observe all the details even if they seem minor and irrelevant at times. This approach will attempt to create something out of where there seems to be nothing.

If you aren't sure which way you should use this idea hack, you can always try both approaches on one creative problem or scenario, just to be sure you aren't overlooking anything.

Best Situations to Use

This will be a helpful idea hack when you have become stuck in seeing a problem as so simple that there is little room to breathe creatively, feeling that you don't have much to work with. In this case, you will use the Detail part of this hack. Or you can use the Abridge part of the hack when there is such great detail, complexity, and depth that you have a hard time figuring out where to start on your creative path.

Example

Consider a scenario where you are a comedian, and you have a whole set of jokes you want to deliver to an audience for a one hour show. You look over at your jokes, and you become upset because you realize they aren't very funny. You have pages and pages of jokes you plan to deliver, and some of the basic ideas are funny, but they just don't land quite right.

You decide to look extra carefully at the details of how your jokes are constructed, and pay attention to the individual word choices you made. Soon enough, you realize the jokes are not bad at all, but on a detailed level you have used words that are not funny enough. The ideas were good, but the final word choices were not the best. Now that you see the problem is one of certain details, you are able to come up with ideas for funny words to fix it.

Exercises to Try

For the following exercises, consider simplifying a complex problem, or looking at the details of a problem that appears simple, as you come up with ideas.

- What are some ideas for new styles of pottery? Examine closely, in great detail, some current styles and patterns of pottery.

    o   Hint: pay attention to materials, patterns, styles, colors, etc.

- What are some ideas for a new business or company? Examine the small processes of day to day businesses.

- What are some ideas for the best vacation spots? Examine the details of some of these hot spots.

- What are some ideas for how to get more people to exercise? Instead of getting lost in the larger problem, look at the details of individuals' lives who struggle with this.

- If you want to create a new material – such as for fabric or a type of tire, closely examine the materials that have been designed by competitors.

Randomness

Description of the Idea Hack

This idea hack will involve finding random ideas to work with. Sometimes we have gone in wrong directions enough times that we no longer trust our own ability to come up with good ideas. Or we simply need access to completely new ideas, ideas so fresh that we aren't really concerned if they are completely relevant. Our minds are quick to find patterns and to create when given stimulation, even random stimulation. Such ideas can be more useful than many of us might think. The point with random ideas is that any stimulus at all is better than nothing. Of course, most of us aren't aware of a random stimulus generating machine. The closest thing we are likely to find is a tool that generates random words or pictures. But these types of tools will suffice, and get us creating new ideas once again.

As you are exposed to new and random ideas, I would urge you to record any that you find interesting or relevant to your problem. If you have any immediate thoughts about how the random word could be useful, then you should write that down as well.

Mostly, the point of this book has been to hack ideas on your own, without the need for outside help. Obviously, this one is an exception and you will receive some outside help. Nonetheless, I believe this is a powerful tool, and that it is worth mentioning and considering in your idea hacking tool belt. Computers and artificial intelligence systems will only become a bigger part of daily life as time passes. It makes sense to be open to using them for idea hacking.

For those still uncertain about this hack, perhaps because it feels like the computer will do all the work, and that the ideas are not yours, this misses the point. When the computer generates the words and concepts, the point will be for you to "piggy-back" off of those ideas and to form your own. Even if you adapt a random idea and turn it into your own, it will still form a new creative idea for you.

Best Situations to Use

This idea hack is useful when you don't know what direction you want your creativity to move in. It can also be worthwhile when you feel completely lost, unsure of what to read, learn, or where to turn to make progress. And of course, it will also help if you have tried many options and nothing has worked.

This hack will help if you are open to completely new and unusual ideas that may take you in entirely unexpected directions. And by the nature of this system, you will need to be patient, to go through some ideas that are irrelevant to what you are trying to accomplish.

Example

First comes the question of how to get random ideas to start with. People will generally not be good at coming up with these. We tend to think in classifications, so if I tell you "fruits", you can come up with many of those. Or if I say "animals", you can come up with many examples of them as well. However, if I say "random ideas", you may actually get stuck, unable to come up with much, or you may find yourself coming up with too many ideas in one area, such as too many location names, for example. But this hack is about sampling quite randomly, as broadly as possible. Instead of coming up with these on your own, I would recommend using an online random word or random concept generator. These will be much more reliable.

For example, with ideagenerator.creativitygames.net, you can generate new words or images. I used the tool to come up with the following random word list:

River, space, pea, wool, ring, caffeine, haystack, holiday, champagne, queue, sail, brass, garden, stream, opera, gossip, donkey, interlude, cucumber, file, salon, spire, scandal, dance, intriguing, **comet**, whale, title, tart, **lipstick**, jury, **plastic**, button, cashier, capsicum, silence, porch, beans, kidnap, granite, tower, trellis, pocket watch, essay, jug, truck, mint, elephant

To get to an example of how to use this idea hack, let's try coming up with a new style of clothing using some of the randomly generated words above. "River" might give us a water theme, to add aquatic and flowing designs onto a skirt or dress, or perhaps to make the clothes itself waterproof. The word "plastic" could make us think of the opposite, of going with biodegradable products that do not harm the environment. "Lipstick" might make us think of going with clothing that does not stain easily. "Comet" (like the cleaner brand) could make us think of clothes that washes easily, and isn't too complicated to clean.

Exercises to Try

For the following exercises, use a random word generator to stimulate you to think in new creative directions. Note that the tools for generating random ideas are available right below this sub-section.

- What are some new ideas for a product or service to create?
- What are some new ideas for song lyrics or a poem?
- What are some new ideas for a multi-purpose type of furniture?
- What are some new ideas for a company brand name or logo design?
- What are some new ideas for a smartphone feature?

Tools to Use

- Random word generator:
  http://www.textfixer.com/tools/random-words.php
- Random word/picture generator:
  http://ideagenerator.creativitygames.net/
- Story plot idea generator:
  http://writers-den.pantomimepony.co.uk/writers-plot-ideas.php
- Idea generator for things to do:
  http://random-idea.com/

Systems / Analogies

Description of the Idea Hack

Whatever domain or system you are working with in your creative problem, compare it to a completely different system from another domain, even if it appears unrelated.

Of course, in order to compare different systems, you will want to have some knowledge of these different areas. If you are not already learning broadly in unique areas, then doing so would be a help to your creativity in general, but will also make you more effective in using certain idea hacks, such as this one.

As some example systems, consider the mechanics of a car, the anatomy and physiology of human beings, the water (weather) cycle, how tectonic plates work, how electricity works, how radio waves travel through space, types and styles of artistic paintings, types of trees, the aqueduct system of ancient Rome, the fighting system in karate, or prison systems, to name some.

Comparing different systems to each other will help you to find unexpected relationships and make a creative breakthrough in your thinking. You don't necessarily need to be the foremost expert in these systems, but you will want to have a solid general knowledge of some systems in order to compare them with each other.

Best Situations to Use

When you notice a similarity between different systems, it will be interesting to explore if there are other ways that they overlap too, or to ask yourself why there are any similarities at all between these systems that are normally thought of as completely different.

Also, this will be a useful idea hack when you suspect it is possible that a problem you regularly face has been solved in another domain, or in another system. Or even if you suspect a problem you regularly face is also common in another area, you may wish to explore what kind of solutions they are coming up with.

In general, this will be a good idea hack to gain a new understanding of how systems that appear to be completely different, may actually have some interesting similarities. Also, systems that appear to be the same on the surface, may actually be completely different when you take a closer look. These unexpected findings between different systems will help to promote your ability to come up with new creative ideas.

Example

In this case, you are an employer, and you are looking for a new creative system to find employees and keep them motivated to continue working with you. You end up watching a documentary on your free time about prison systems. This helps you to realize that for a prisoner to be released, there are many processes which must take place – evaluations, parole, counseling, etc.

You come to understand that you have mostly been choosing employees just based on their prior work experience, but often you end up with people who do not like the job and end up quitting. You decide that you could use the prison system as an analogy to make your own improvements, to keep more workers. But you would apply what you learned in a different way. Instead of having so many criteria to release your workers (as they do in prison), you could increase your criteria to hire the workers, to make sure they are the right ones, and are more likely to stay.

Your idea is to have them read a pamphlet that explains all of the things that will be required of them on the job and what to expect, so they do not become easily dissatisfied and leave. They will also have a formal mentor for their first year on the job. This will make the transition go smoothly. You will then encourage open communication between the new hire and management so that any questions or concerns are taken care of quickly, rather than building up.

All you have done here is take the idea that it is not a simple and easy process to be released from prison, and turned it around so that it is not a simple and easy process to be accepted into your employee positions.

Exercises to Try

For the following exercises, consider how one system compares to another as you come up with ideas.

- How does the water cycle compare to a problem you've been working on?

    o Hint: the water cycle involves water vapor rising up to form clouds, rain water forming and dropping down then running down to oceans and lakes, the accumulation of water on the ground and oceans, and then the water vapor rising up again.

- How does the human organ system compare to a problem you've been working on?

- How does agriculture and farming compares to a problem you've been working on?

- How do computer systems (perhaps memory storage or processing speed) compare to a problem you've been working on?

- How does your country's political system compare to others?

Diffusion / De-focus

Description of the Idea Hack

Sometimes, a high amount of focus can actually work against us. Of course, most of the time a laser-beam intense focus is helpful for making something of high quality and for being productive. But sometimes you are in a new and uncertain creative territory. It may not be clear exactly what you should be focusing on, so to focus too deeply on any one thing can become a mistake, causing you to miss better opportunities that are more worthy of your attention.

When in these uncertain situations, one strategy is to diffuse your focus, to allow an unfocused calm to come over you. Rather than to feel certain that you know the best path, allow your mind to diffuse, and scatter its attention to other things, not just the one thing you believe is important. Allow it to stay completely open, and drift toward anything new that comes along. That new thing may be highly relevant to solving the creative issue.

Your mind will then be able to take into consideration a variety of ideas that seem to have no real significance. The key word is they *seem* to have no significance, which is why they are easily overlooked, but when your mind diffuses, it values all things as being possibly relevant and important. The creative mindset is often able to redefine the way you look at a problem. Having too much focus on a narrow area, and being too rigid in your viewpoints, is not going to help you come up with creative ideas. You are more likely to get stuck or go down a misguided path, this way.

To practice a diffusion of thought can be difficult for those of us who are orderly and systematic and clearly focused on specific goals. These are good qualities, but are worth setting aside sometimes when we want to come up with creative ideas. Keep in mind that I wouldn't suggest always being in a diffuse state of mind. Rather, it is a technique to use. In that sense, your focused mind should guide the use of this technique when it appears to be worthwhile. With concrete and direct problems, diffusion of thought may slow you down and annoy others, rather than help the situation. This idea hack wouldn't be recommended with normal problems, but it is recommended with creative problems or when you want to come up with new ideas.

To enter a diffusion of thought, allow your train of thought to become loose, illogical even, straying from one thought to another rapidly. You will be making loose peripheral observations and associations. You may create an idea-chain on paper to see where your ideas start, and where they end up. You will likely see that the ideas jump around in unpredictable and interesting ways. By idea chain, I mean you start off with one concept, then another enters the mind, and that one makes you think of another, and so on. Each idea makes you think of another idea, but you do not force yourself to stay focused on one theme.

Best Situations to Use

When you have become so focused on a task that you are only looking at a very small space. Especially if you have done this and are making little progress creatively and in coming up with new ideas. This system will help you look outside of the small space, or box that you have limited yourself to.

Example

Imagine a scenario where you are a publicist for a famous novelist who writes stories about talking animals, and the publisher is pressuring you to come up with a new and interesting way to market the book. You are a bit stressed about whether you will be able to come up with something, so you decide to go for a walk in the park to get your mind off of marketing.

Rather than being 100% focused on your problem, you go for a walk and allow your focus to wander to the environment or other thoughts unrelated to the novel you are to help promote. In the back of your mind though, of course your subconscious won't let go of the problem you have, to find a new way to market this novelist's work.

As you walk, you enjoy the scenery. The weather is sunny, the flowers are blooming, and young people are tossing Frisbees and laughing and having a good time. You also enjoy the fact that people are walking their dogs, who are having a good time running around in the open.

Then, you notice a small dog with a shirt on, sized specifically for that dog. You think it's funny how much people love their dogs, where they even dress them like humans. You laugh and move on. A moment later, of course you remember that the novel you are publicizing has talking dogs, cats, and other animals as its main heroes. Then the idea hits you – to print t-shirts with an ad for the book, for pets to wear. Then you can sell or give them away as a marketing tool. The pet owners will walk them through the park, and many people will see it since the weather is nice and people are spending time outdoors.

You have solved your problem and come up with a new and likely effective way to market the book.

Exercises to Try

Try the following techniques to reach a state of de-focus as you solve creative problems. The objective is to direct your mind toward an unfocused, flowing state, rather than rigid and overly focused on one thing.

- Practice meditation or mindfulness.

- Try breathing exercises.

- Go for a calming walk.

- Allow your mind to drift naturally, to go into a day-dream state.

- Look at something (or experience something) that often prompts you into thinking of another time period or era where times were different, perhaps a time you enjoyed greatly – this could be music, a painting, or a special activity.

For more ways to exercise your creativity, there is a bonus of "101 Creative Exercises to Try" at the end of this book. The next section concludes the book, *Final Tips & Reminders.*

Final Tips & Reminders

If You Struggle to Make Idea Hacks Work for You...

Some of the following are summaries of what has already been stated. Some are new things to consider to help you make the best use of the above idea hacks. I truly want this book and the hacks to work as well for you as they have for me. In order for you to make the best use of the systems discussed, you should be aware that often to come up with ideas, especially good ones, you will want to combine idea hacks with other creativity-boosting strategies. The following are some of the more important points to keep in mind.

Gain expertise

The more experience you gain, the more you will develop a full understanding of how an area works. It is very important for you to understand a topic well before you can make meaningful creations within the domain. You do not need to have the highest amount of expertise, but you should prioritize developing a solid understanding. The most creative people tend to have a moderate amount of expertise in their topic, but they aren't necessarily a leading expert in the field.

Gain a broad range of knowledge

Learning broadly in areas outside of your expertise will help you to come up with new interesting ideas that you can connect to your main field. Those with a broad understanding of many different areas will tend to be more creative. This can be accomplished by traveling, reading in a wide range of topics, and communicating with people who have varied experiences and backgrounds. You want to focus on your expertise of course, but you also want to consider outside ideas you might be able to use creatively in your main area.

Improve your memory

Memory is more related to creativity than you may realize. If you feel that you can rarely come up with any ideas, even simple ideas, it could help to work on exercising your memory. Keep in mind that creative people are often simply remembering prior ideas they have heard, and noticing that it interconnects with something else. Remembering is one part of coming up with the idea, then noticing that the idea appropriately connects with other areas, is another part of the process.

If you would like to improve your memory, there are many books available which cover the topic.

Document your dreams

Writing down your dreams will help to remind you that you are creative, even if it doesn't feel that way sometimes. Also, your dreams may give you wild and interesting ideas, some of which actually may apply to your real world problems. Many creative people have written their dreams, so this could be a useful way to jumpstart your creative ideas.

Forget about great ideas

Give up the need to create something great, or the next big thing. Grant yourself permission to come up with bad ideas that lead nowhere. Eventually, you will hit upon great ideas if you allow yourself to get the bad ones out of your system.

It's very common for people to shy away from being creative because they feel that they are bad at it. But this is as silly as thinking that you are bad at dreaming. We all dream and create in our sleep, and some of us may have more interesting or creative ideas than others, but we are all capable of being creative.

Let go of the fear of being wrong with your creative ideas. They can be no more wrong than your dreams can be. We get too used to being graded in school, but for this first stage of creativity, quantity will be more important than quality. Allow the ideas to flow out of you, regardless if you feel they are good or not.

Surround yourself with creative people

Creative people tend to build ideas off of other ideas. You will find that there is a sort of compounding power to creative ideas. If they come up with idea after idea about something, you will soon find yourself wondering about different directions and come up with your own possibilities. There will be a contagious part about it, where their enthusiasm and idea building tends to rub off on others. Often, their creativity starts with curiosity in asking about everything. Many of those questions will lead to creative directions. For example, they may ask something like "Why don't we try doing it this way?" or "Is there a reason this wouldn't work?", but this is after asking more fundamental questions to understand a problem fully.

From complaint to creation

I think this is something we all experience regularly. You receive a product or service, or otherwise have some kind of experience that goes horribly wrong. You think, "I can't believe that was such a failure. How could they get everything wrong? Anyone can see there are A, B, C, and so forth problems with this. Why don't they just change this or that and it will solve everything." Many of us though, don't actually offer any solutions. All we have is a complaint.

Something I have learned, in my creations and in spending time with other creators, is there are many, many complaints about virtually everything. Look up your favorite movies or products, for example and read the negative reviews. You may be surprised that a movie you love is hated deeply by others. Yet how many of these complainers have ever created something of their own?

Complaining is actually a good skill to have. This is not the problem. We all need to be able to judge poor quality, and have the right to vocalize it when we notice it. But I would challenge you to catch yourself complaining. Don't stop yourself, you can keep going until you're done. And when you are done complaining about something that has gone horribly wrong, ask what can be done to fix it. Is this a chance to create something new? Perhaps you have a solution that is immensely better than the current ones available? Don't let your complaints go wasted, see how you can turn them into new creations.

Shield yourself from negative criticisms to start

Early on in your creative goals, protect yourself from negative criticisms to get yourself motivated to start. Too much criticism will make you lose motivation early on, so avoid it entirely as you get started.

However, realize that as you make creative progress, getting closer to finishing a product or service, that getting feedback will be important to polish up your creation and make it the best that you possibly can.

Wanting to be creative isn't enough to make it happen. Use "Idea Hacks" to make it happen.

I have heard of many people who would wish to be more creative, to get more ideas, to make something happen. Like with anything else, to actually be creative requires taking action. Many people do not know where to begin, and so they get stuck and give up. This book was made to help keep you from feeling stuck, and for those who were not sure where to begin on their creative journey.

I would encourage you to use idea hacks to come up with many, many ideas, perhaps even hundreds of them. It's important to get out those bad ideas first to start coming up with the good ones. Perhaps your first hundred will be bad, and maybe some of your next hundred after that will be good, then some of the next hundred will be excellent. Take some of those excellent ideas, and start a plan to turn them into a reality.

However, don't put too much pressure on yourself when you start. Your creations or ideas don't need to result in life changing or ground-breaking things. Perhaps eventually they will, but allow yourself to aim for small goals to begin with. The important thing is to build up your ideas and start creating. The evaluation process and implementation are easy to get stuck on, but the smaller your projects are the more easily you will overcome those hurdles. Allow yourself to have some small creative wins so that you can gradually move up to larger and larger creations.

Idea Hacks Made this Book Possible

As a last point, this feels like the appropriate time to state that much of this book was created by my direct use of idea hacks. Since my favorite idea hack is the Alphabet one, I often ran through this system to try to come up with an exhaustive list of idea hacks, which led me to come up with many of those present in this book.

To me, this is an extra validation that the systems truly work. However, I am willing to do what all creators will have to do. I will put my creation (this book) out there and let it be judged by the masses. It is very possible some idea hacks will work better for you than others. However, I predict that most people will find at least some of these hacks to be highly useful in their personal case, which was all I could hope to achieve.

I hope you found something useful here that you can apply in your life.

Thank You

Thank you for taking the time to read *Idea Hacks*. I hope that you found the information useful. Just remember that a key part of the learning process is putting what you read into practice.

Before you go, I want to invite you to pick up your free copy of *Step Up Your Learning: Free Tools to Learn Almost Anything*. All you have to do type this link into your browser:

http://bit.ly/Robledo

Also, if you have any questions, comments, or feedback about this book, you can send me a message and I'll get back to you as soon as possible. Please put the title of the book you are commenting on in the subject line. My email address is:

ic.robledo@mentalmax.net

Did You Learn Something New?

If you found value in this book, please review it on Amazon so I can stay focused on writing more great books. Even a short one or two sentences would be helpful.

To go directly to the review page, you may type this into your web browser:

http://hyperurl.co/86ht2a

An Invitation to the "Master Your Mind" Community (on Facebook)

I founded a community where we can share advice or tips on our journey to mastering the mind. Whether you want to be a better learner, improve your creativity, get focused, or work on other such goals, this will be a place to find helpful information and a supportive network. I hope you join us and commit to taking your mind to a higher level.

To go directly to the page to join the community, you may type this into your web browser:

http://hyperurl.co/xvbpfc

More Books by I. C. Robledo

The Secret Principles of Genius

The Intellectual Toolkit of Geniuses

The Smart Habit Guide

55 Smart Apps to Level Up Your Brain

No One Ever Taught Me How to Learn

Ready, Set, Change

To see the full list of authored books, visit:

www.Amazon.com/author/icrobledo

Bonus: 101 Creative Exercises to Try

1. What would aliens look like? What would they feed off of? Would they be logical, chaotic, intelligent, or mindless?

2. Answer a question Google has asked in job interviews – How many golf balls can fit on a school bus?

3. Write song lyrics.

4. Do something you do every day, but do it in a way you've never done it before.

5. Predict what the world will be like in 20 years.

6. Challenge the nature of reality and question if you are in a dream now. What is the difference between dreams and reality?

7. Consider the viability of something no one else would probably even give a second thought to.

8. Experience something fantastical and otherworldly like *Gulliver's Travels*, *Alice in Wonderland*, or *Lord of the Rings*.

9. Allow yourself to be messy. Research has shown messy (or disorderly) people are more creative.

10. Come up with your own objects, people, or figures that you can see in the stars at night (instead of the famous ones like Big Dipper, Little Dipper, Orion, etc.).

11. For something that is too obvious, brainstorm an alternative explanation.

12. When in a public space with strangers, create a narrative for what someone is doing. Why are they there? Why is their mood what it is?

13. Practice meditation or mindfulness.

14. Read an article or book that you normally would not read.

15. Network with people in broad unrelated domains.

16. Document your dreams.

17. Practice drawing or painting.

18. Create your own board game.

19. Compose music – you may use the assistance of music apps.

20. Practice free association – Sigmund Freud would have a list of words, and then you would come up with the first thing that comes to mind based off of it.

21. Network with creative people.

22. Write a short story, micro-fiction, novel, or poem.

23. Pick up a new hobby.

24. Engage with other cultures - their art, music, beliefs, traditions, etc.

25. Seek rounded out knowledge on many topics.

26. Push yourself to improvise something on the spot - a song, a poem, a drawing - don't over-think it.

27. Join Toastmasters and give a speech.

28. Join an improvisational group – for comedy or drama, for example.

29. Practice thinking of alternative uses for everyday objects - don't get trapped into functional fixation, of only seeing objects as performing the one function they were intended for.

30. Use clay (or something similar) to create mini-sculptures.

31. Rather than wait to answer someone else's questions, generate your own.

32. Practice taking alternate perspectives.

33. Take the time to define problems, rather than jumping in right away.

34. Be aware of clichés. Don't idly say exactly what you have always heard. Consider new signature ways to get your message across.

35. Get to the point of almost solving a creative problem, and then don't. Just let it simmer in the background, so your subconscious can handle it - perhaps taking a nap or a break to let your mind wander.

36. Instead of "Why?" ask "Why not?"

37. Look and observe as if seeing for the first time, as a newborn.

38. Practice using your imagination in the dark to see people, figures, and objects come to life.

39. Keep asking "Why?", or stating "Because..." to go deeper and deeper into the origins of a creative problem.

40. Find an arch nemesis, to forever keep you on your toes – needing to out-compete and out-create them.

41. Do a wildly challenging activity, like NaNoWriMo – which stands for National novel writing month, where the goal is to write a 50,000 word full novel in just one month.

42. Meet people around the world virtually – through online apps or tools such as Skype.

43. Play with a young child, they are masters of original thinking and will want to pretend.

44. Choose random words and find an association between them.

45. Be the social chameleon. Practice getting along in any social setting.

46. Go back in time and change something (in your mind). How would the results change?

47. Study natural life solutions to problems - flight, swimming, etc.

48. Don't look up answers so fast to your questions (Googling it). Let your mind run wild with possibilities (What if... type responses).

49. Invent something new – You don't necessarily need to get a patent on it, but why not if you feel so inclined. It may simply be a new process, and not necessarily a product.

50. Come up with 5 ideas about something - business, potential inventions, story ideas, ways to get healthier, etc.

51. Do something completely untypical for you - visit a new place, try a new hobby, hang out with new people, etc.

52. Encourage creativity by blurring the lines of what is appropriate or acceptable in a situation.

53. Write a comedy routine as if you were a stand-up comic, or create a comic strip.

54. Celebrate or learn about a holiday you know little about.

55. Give yourself an extra challenge – such as adding a time constraint or trying to accomplish more with a project than you would normally handle.

56. Try juggling.

57. Take something apart and put it together again.

58. Imagine alternate possibilities that may have happened in your life – where else might you be if things had gone differently?

59. Create a symphony in your mind, or some kind of arrangement of music.

60. Consider the self-imposed limits you create for yourself, and stretch beyond it.

61. Create a children's game (like "Duck, Duck, Goose", "Hide and Seek", etc.).

62. Create a piece of artwork (painting, pottery, sculpture, etc.).

63. Listen to music and visualize your own music video for the song (not one that already exists for it).

64. Create a story by filling in every other word, with friends.

65. Take household items and brainstorm how to improve them.

66. Take everyday items and brainstorm how they could be used as weapons.

67. Travel somewhere new.

68. Play an instrument.

69. Look at stains on walls, or the clouds in the sky, and ask what the images could be (e.g., toaster, car, plane, etc.).

70. Pay attention to smells for inspiration.

71. Look to randomness - explore a random page in a book store, a random street you've never taken, or talk to a random person.

72. Connect facts from different and unrelated fields.

73. Learn a foreign language (may include hieroglyphics, sign language, braille, etc.)

74. Play the role of participant observer, where you enter a situation and observe it as if you were an objective researcher, learning how a certain people (or animals) interact and how they live.

75. Watch a conversation from afar, and fill in what you think they are saying, or make it up.

76. Get in a chair, and refuse to get up until you come up with 20 new ideas.

77. Cook by mixing new ingredients you've never used, or old ingredients in a new mixture you've never tried.

78. Color in a coloring book (there are some adult coloring books too), or draw a figure that could be colored in.

79. Return to a childhood passion, or one from your younger days.

80. Ask 10 questions about something.

81. Practice thinking in another language.

82. Simply imagine - your ideal place, friend, vacation, or job, etc.

83. Create a character sketch for a book or movie.

84. Use online free creative artistic tools for fun (such as Gimp).

85. Use idle or downtime to create something or come up with ideas, don't waste it.

86. Make a creative haven environment that helps inspire you to create, perhaps a room filled with interesting music, pictures, or art to get you in the mood.

87. Think about what you want to create, right before you go to bed. Then put it into action when you wake up the next day.

88. Perform a physical exercise that depletes your energy completely to help clear your mind and get ready to create something new.

89. Set a time to be creative, to make this a daily habit.

90. Change up a routine – such as start driving a new route to work, start a new exercise habit, or something else.

91. Create your own ending – watch a movie or read a book up to close to the ending, then put it aside and invent your own ending for what you think happens, or should happen. This may be especially interesting with murder mysteries or with *Scooby-Doo* type shows.

92. Invent stories as you are falling asleep. Can be fantasy versions of your own life, or dramatic productions.

93. Create your ideal life. How would the day go? Where would you live? Who would you associate with?

94. When you have a big problem, brainstorm 100 ways to solve it before you go checking Google or asking friends about it.

95. Learn how things actually work in the real world, beyond just a textbook explanation – such as how televisions, computers, cars, or radios work.

96. Start something without needing to know the end point. Embrace the exhilaration of not knowing.

97. Find some common item you consume regularly, and make it for yourself - toothpaste, mouthwash, laundry detergent, juice, etc.

98. For a creative problem, ask what you would do if you were someone completely unlike you.

99. Invent a new word for a concept, like "Ubuntu", a word from the South African region literally meaning human-ness. It is often used to mean "the belief in a universal bond of sharing that connects all humanity".

100. Allow yourself to get lost and have an adventure.

101. Hold conflicting thoughts simultaneously. Stretch yourself to see how two opposite viewpoints can both be true.

Made in the USA
Lexington, KY
06 December 2017